POLYAMORY:

Easy Introductory Guide to Polyamorous Relationships

MARISSA BLAKE

© Copyright 2019 BY MARISSA BLAKE.

All rights reserved. This book may not be reproduced, or transmitted in any form electronic, mechanical, photocopy, recording, or otherwise, without the prior permission of the author. It is illegal to copy this book, post it to a website, or distribute it by any other means without permission.

Neither the publisher nor the author is engaged in rendering legal or any other professional service through this book. If expert assistance is required, the services of appropriate professionals should be sought. The publisher and the author shall have neither liability nor responsibility to any person or entity with respect to any loss or damage caused directly or indirectly by the professional by using information in this book.

Easy Introductory Guide to Polyamorous Relationships i

Awakening 1

Chapter One 3

What is polyamory? 3

    What Can Poly Mean for a Man's Penis? 5

    How Can a Man Protect His Poly-Active Penis? 7

Chapter Two 9

History of Polyamory 9

Chapter Three 26

Reasons Why Polyamory Does Work 26

Chapter Four 32

How to Transition From Monogamy to Polyamory 32

    Polyamory and the Penis 34

    Stigma of Polyamorous Relationships 34

    Why Monogamy is Unnatural & Responsible Non-Monogamy Can Save a Relationship 37

    Monogamy and Infidelity 42

Chapter Five 53

The Future of Love and Relationships 53

    Vision of a New Morality 55

Chapter Six 64

Jealousy in Relatioships 64

    Handling Jealousy in Relationships 66

    So, how do you handle this jealousy thing? 69

    How to build a relationship without jealousy............. 72

Chapter Seven 101

Communication in Relationships: Is it really important?
.... 101

    Communication as the Number One rule of polyamory
    104

Chapter Eight... 122

How to quit worrying and love your partner's other
partners... 122

Awakening

I recently went to the Museum of Sex in NYC and saw an exhibit about the sex life of animals. Of the many fascinating facts I discovered, the most surprising was that of all the animals scientists believed to be monogamous, none really were. Many had long term socially monogamous partners, but the sex was a free for all. Using DNA testing, scientists determined that up to 97% of all offspring in supposed monogamous relationships were created by EPC, or extra pair coupling.

Then last week Newsweek ran an article about polyamory, featuring a group of two women and three men who were managing to have a number of relationships between them. One of the women lived with two of the men and was legally married to one of them, and the other was married to the third man. They spoke openly about what was necessary for it to work, and I was struck by how conscious they all seemed to be.

It got me thinking about consciousness, sexuality and relationships. Most of us are not ready for the honesty, transparency and humility that are necessary to make polyamory work. When I say humility, I mean being able to look at your own jealousies and insecurities with a gentle eye and a willingness to speak your truth with love. It takes a really conscious person to be willing to expose themselves in that way. The group interviewed by Newsweek spoke at length about the insecurities that arise and how everyone deals with them.

Some would say that with that much consciousness, a person would be more inclined to be monogamous. That's one possibility, and is more socially acceptable than polyamory. To play devil's advocate for a moment, at a certain level of consciousness the awareness arises that we are all one, and that love is all that's real. When this awareness lodges in your entire being rather than just being a thought in your brain, perceptions shift. Societal norms become less important and the desire to judge others disappears.

We can't pretend that we're innately monogamous as a species. Some of us are more inclined toward monogamy than others, but our level of consciousness does not dictate an inclination for or against monogamy. At lower levels of consciousness, people have affairs.

At higher levels, they consider an open relationship or polyamory.

Chapter One

What is polyamory?

There are tons of synonyms for polyamory. Everything from the classic 'open relationship' to 'ethical non-monogamy' (not that it's always ethical), which are both a flavor of polyamory but not necessarily the end all be all. What is boils down to is this: when a person is polyamorous (let's use poly for short), he is open to the idea of having loving relationships with more than one person at a time. Now, this doesn't mean a man's penis is on overload, having sex multiple times each day.

Poly is largely misunderstood because of the focus on the sex part of it. People can be in a relationship with just one partner and be polyamorous (so long as the partner knows and agrees - otherwise, it's just called cheating). Some poly players don't have sex with anyone other than their partner, but have loving, romantic relationships with other people. Some people just have multiple relationships going all at once. It's a pretty individualized concept around a core belief.

Polyamory is a relationship model in which one or both partners in a relationship are consensually non-monogamous, meaning they can date - and yes, even have sex - with others. Of course, this typically begs the question, 'Well, isn't that just like swinging or going to wife-swap sex parties?' No, not at all, actually. What we've discovered is that whenever people who are new to the idea of poly first encounter the topic, the first thing they focus on is the idea of having sex with new partners.

The thing that blows their minds is when we tell them that poly doesn't even have to involve sex. It can, but it does not have to, because poly is about love first and foremost. But the one thing that can be said without backpedaling is that poly is not for everyone. Determining if it's for you is where things can get dicey, because there is no test you can take that will tell you if poly is right for you.

Polyamory, like any relationship model, has its success stories and its horror stories. In the world of monogamy, roughly 50 percent of all new marriages fail, according to recent studies. Gay marriages haven't been well enough defined or documented for any kind of definitive study about their rate of longevity, either. So, our view is that people are what make a relationship - from any model - good or bad. But choosing which way you want to go has a lot to do with how certain elements of relationships make you feel.

So, short of being able to give you a guide to determining if poly is right for you, here are some things to think about before you put up a profile on an alternative lifestyle dating service.

- **Jealousy:**

Are you the jealous type? Does your blood boil when you see your partner paying attention to someone in a flirtatious manner? Does imagining your partner with someone else make you absent-mindedly wander the ammo aisle at Walmart? If so, poly may be a bit of a longshot for you.

- **Insecurity:**

Are you afraid that your partner will leave you for someone else 'better' than you? Do you sometimes have feelings that you don't deserve your partner, or that he or she could easily do better? When you are home alone, are you afraid that your partner is spending time with someone else behind your back?

Chances are that you should not only leave the idea of poly on the backburner, but you and your partner should also seek help to deal with those feelings of insecurity. Insecurity is a threat to maintaining a stable monogamous relationship, but it is a nuclear bomb that can devastate a poly relationship.

- **Time:**

Are you busy? We mean, really busy? Three jobs, soccer parents, caregivers and Red Cross volunteers kind of busy? While you might have the right mindset and heart to open yourself and your relationship to poly, you may not have the time. Remember, poly is about new relationships, not just hook-ups, and any relationship worth pursuing is worth the time to properly dedicate to it. If you are a couple who barely have time for each other, then poly might not be the best bet for you until you can open up the calendar.

What Can Poly Mean for a Man's Penis?

While it doesn't seem to be an immediate connection, there are several things a man should consider from a sex and penis health standpoint. Here are a few concerns a man should be cognizant of when practicing his desired form of poly:

- **Disease:**

This is a no brainer. There are tons of sexually transmitted infections (STIs) out there that can maim and kill. There are also other ones that can stick around forever and require disclosures to partners each and every time sex is had.

- **Infections:**

It's not only STIs that can be transmitted intimately. Things like yeast infections and urinary tract infections can also find their way to an otherwise healthy penis.

- **Guilt Dick:**

Some guys have a hard time sleeping with someone (or many ones) else when in an otherwise committed relationship. This can result in a failure to get or maintain an erection. Psychology and the penis have an intense relationship, and a lot can factor in to that.

- **Allergens:**

Seems weird to talk about, but men (and their respective penises) can be allergic to certain bed linens, perfumes, and other cleaning and grooming products used by multiple partners.

How Can a Man Protect His Poly-Active Penis?

There are several ways a man can stay healthy and active in a sexual poly lifestyle with a penis that performs well on command. Here are a few tips for how to keep penis health central while playing poly:

- **Use Condoms and Other Barrier Methods:**

Don't use the same toys with one partner that are used with another. Get tested regularly. You know all this, but it's worth mentioning. Also, bring your own condoms.

- **Have a Straightforward Sex Talk With All New Partners:**

This should include any disease states, infections going on, overall health, and consent. Discuss all potential sexual practices, but be sure to be specific about anything that might injure the penis, such as cock rings, certain positions, and long nails.

- **Have an Emotional Check-in:**

For men who have iffy feelings about a poly lifestyle, a check-in or regular appointment with a sex therapist isn't a bad idea. This will help a man keep his mental game in check, so it doesn't affect his penis.

- **Urinate After Sex:**

This cleans everything out and can protect against bacteria and infection.

- **Keep the Penis Clean and Healthy:**

Be sure to thoroughly wash the penis daily, and after any sexual escapades, with warm water and a gentle cleanser. Rinse well and air dry. After cleaning the skin, use a specially formulated penis health creme on the penis.

Choose a crème with tons of vitamins and nutrients that protect and rejuvenate the penis, like vitamins A, B, C, and D. L-carnitine is also a worthy ingredient to look for, as it protects against peripheral nerve damage that can affect a penis's prowess over time.

So, now you know what poly is and how it can affect your penis. Keep these considerations in mind to ensure that you have a healthy and fulfilling emotional and sexual life.

Chapter Two

History of Polyamory

Relationships of some form of non-monogamy have been around for as long as human civilization has been around, some of which were even honest, multi-partner relationships and not cheating. Today's concept of monogamous, nuclear families is a very recent development ... within just this last century! It is important to note that 'it has always been so' is not a good enough reason, by itself, to continue doing anything. But it is false to say that monogamy has 'always been so', because the fact is, it hasn't.

In the Ecotopian Encyclopedia, Ernest Callenbach contends, 'In the long sweep of human history, the nuclear family will probably be seen as a very brief aberration, brought about by the special needs of industrial capitalism and the isolated suburban living made possible by cars, but insufficient for nurturing and supporting human beings.

In [communes and extended families] we will approximate the ancient groupings our species has relied on for survival: small bands whose variety of strengths and talents give great resilience against outside threats, and whose interior psychological life is rich and complicated enough to challenge its members' developmental potentials.'

Polygyny, the most common form of Polgyamy, is widely practiced in many African cultures and countries. Fraternal Polyandry, where one woman is married to brothers, is traditionally practiced among nomadic Tibetans including Nepal and parts of China.

Ancient Mesopotamia was originally a matriarchal society guided by a female Goddess, Ishtar, who was the ruler of everything including war and weapons. After victories, women in her temples would celebrate with feasting and sex. When male gods arose and power shifted towards men, the temple became a house of prostitution, however the prostitutes were considered 'holy'.

All women were required to go to the Temple of Ishtar at least once in their lives (usually after they were married) to sit in the temple until a stranger came and threw a piece of silver into her lap. Then she had to leave the temple and have sex with him. Only then could she return home. Also in Mesopotamia was the Peor cult, which was mainly a public orgy that began with an exhibitionist show of people engaged in various sexual acts. The finale included the audience and bestiality was also part of the show. In this most early of civilizations, we find some of the first references to sexually transmitted diseases: gonorrhea and syphilis.

In Ancient Egypt, pretty much any sexual practice was accepted and condemned at one point or another. During one period, a woman could go into the Temple of Amun and have sex with anyone she wanted until menstruation. Then followed a celebration. After that she was married.

Throughout the thousands of years of Chinese history, it was common for rich Chinese men to have a wife and various concubines. Before the establishment of the People's Republic of China, it was lawful to have a wife and multiple concubines within Chinese marriage. Emperors, government officials and rich merchants had up to hundreds of concubines after marrying their first wives.

During the Chou dynasty (770 - 222 BC), female homosexuality was widespread, but male homosexuality was forbidden. For a brief time, it was believed that female prostitutes had acquired more 'yin' than other women because they had sex with so many men and therefore men could gain more yin from prostitutes than normal women. Then Chinese doctors discovered STDs and began warning men against prostitutes.

220 BC - 24 AD, the Ch'in Dynasty saw sex as only for procreation, but allowed men to see concubines with an entire set of Confucianist rules governing the practice. Confucianism also claimed that the ability to manage a family that included more than one wife and set of children was part of the steps of learning for spiritual growth.

With the return of Taoist doctrines after centuries of war and unrest, during the Sui Dynasty in 590 - 618 AD, Chinese males once again desired many sexual relations with women.

675 BC, the Ionians settled into the North Aegean Islands. Their rulers were polygynists.

During the 4th Century BC, the Etruscans of Italy were described to have the women giving themselves to men that were not their husbands and participating in some sort of public orgy with drink and a feast, after which all the men and women watched each other having sex and swapped partners. The women engaged in gymnastic sexual positions with the men.

The women had no way of knowing who the fathers of their children were because they had sex with different men but there were no illegitimate children in their society. That suggests matrilineal lineage of children if the women were allowed to have multiple partners with no worry of illegitimacy of their children.

The Torah (what Christians know as The Old Testament) includes specific regulations regarding polygamy, including: Exodus 21:10, which states that multiple marriages are not to diminish the status of the first wife; Deuteronomy 21:15-17, which states that a man must award the inheritance due to a first-born son to the son who was actually born first, even if he hates that son's mother and likes another wife more; and Deuteronomy 17:17, which states that the king shall not have too many wives.

One source of polygamy was the practice of levirate marriage, where a man was required to marry and support his deceased brother's widow. Usually, however, only leaders and rich men had several wives. Some examples are: Esau, Isaac's son had two wives; Jacob had two wives; Gideon had many wives and 70 sons; King David had several wives; King Solomon had many wives; King Rehoboam had 18 wives and 60 concubines.

Poor men were allowed concubines which sometimes consisted of sex and children with their wives' handmaids, however many men would simply purchase a concubine from the girl's father. Sarah gave Abraham her handmaid when she was unable to have children. Rachel gave Jacob her handmaid. Hannah gave her husband her handmaid and from that sexual encounter came Samuel.

According to traditional Islamic law, a man may take up to four wives, and each of those wives must have her own property, assets, and dowry. Usually the wives have little to no contact with each other and lead separate, individual lives in their own houses, and sometimes in different cities, though they all share the same husband. Thus, polygamy is traditionally restricted to men who can manage things, and in some countries it is illegal for a man to marry multiple wives if he is unable to afford to take care of each of them properly.

The Laws of Manu, in India, allow for a husband to 'seek pleasure elsewhere' with no retribution, however should a wife 'violate the duty which she owes to her lord, the king shall cause her to be devoured by dogs in a place frequented by many'.

In Ancient Greece, the following passage is found in the Oration against Neaera: 'We keep mistresses for our pleasures, concubines for constant attendance, and wives to bear us legitimate children and to be our faithful housekeepers.' Wives had virtually no freedom for sexual or romantic expression. Men could choose from any number of acceptable partners, like wife and concubine, including young boys.

The Roman Empire allowed men to marry women at 12 whether she had reached puberty or not, to engage in adultery, to have sex with prostitutes, concubines and slaves, and to rape women. Wives had no sexual rights and were obligated to submit to their husbands, however prostitutes had more freedoms.

North American Tribal marriage practices vary from tribe to tribe, but the majority of tribes practice some form of polygyny. All sexual practices can be found throughout the tribes, including polygny, polyandry, wife-swapping, premarital sex, extramarital sex, and monogamy, however it is rare that monogamy is the sole sexual practice found in any given tribe.

Under Queen Eleanor's reign (beginning 1122 AD), France & England enjoyed cultured courts, including a Court of Love, which strictly codified and promoted courtly love. The Court of Love specifically claimed that love can exist only in affairs, not marriage. The advent of Courtly Love introduced the elements of emotional love between men and women for the first time, where love was based on mutual relationships of respect and admiration.

During the 16th Century, Queen Marguerite of France was involved in intense but platonic love affairs with 12 men simultaneously. She also wrote stories of platonic and 'perfect' love intermingled with orgies, incestuousness, partner swapping, sexually insatiable priests, etc.

In 1532, Dr. Martin Luther claimed that Jesus probably committed adultery with Mary Magdalene and that sexual impulses were both natural and irrepressible.

'On February 14, 1650, the parliament at Nürnberg decreed that because so many men were killed during the Thirty Years' War, the churches for the following ten years could not admit any man under the age of 60 into a monastery. Priests and ministers not bound by any monastery were allowed to marry. Lastly, the decree stated that every man was allowed to marry up to ten women. The men were admonished to behave honorably, provide for their wives properly, and prevent animosity among them.' Larry O. Jensen, A Genealogical Handbook of German Research (Rev. Ed., 1980) p. 59

17th Century England had a legal term that referred to a person with three spouses, implying that it was common enough to have a law making it illegal - 'Trigamy'.

Diary entries dating back to Medieval times through the 19th Century speak of 'love' for neighbors, cousins and fellow church members more often than spouses. In fact, when honeymoons became popular in the 19th Century, couples often took along friends and family members for company. Victorian men wrote plainly about bedding down with a male friend and expressing love for each other, while Victorian women routinely kicked their husbands out of bed to accommodate a visiting female friend or relative, spending the night kissing, cuddling and pouring out their most intimate thoughts.

In 1831, Joseph Smith began the Church of Latter Day Saints which sanctioned polgyny as 'plural marriage' or 'celestial marriage'. The church's practice of polygamy was not recorded until 1843 and remained a secret practice until 1852. In 1890, in an attempt to gain statehood for Utah, the church officially denounced polygamy, although the annexation didn't happen until 1896. A sect known as Fundamental Mormonism continues to practice polygyny in secret. The official LDS Church does not recognize this sect as part of the Morman Church.

In the mid 1800s, one of the most famous Polyamorous communities came about called the Oneida Community in New York. It was founded by John Humphry Noyes who asserted a doctrine of Perfectionism, which basically claimed that a man reached a state of sinlessness or perfection upon conversion. In his community, he taught 'Mutual Criticism', 'Complex Marriage', and 'Male Continence'. In 1848, he purchased 23 acres of land in Oneida, New York and his group grew to 87 people.

The Oneida Community was a self-supporting agricultural and industrial community. They had a working farm and a sawmill, grew and canned fruits and vegetables, produced silk thread, and manufactured animal traps, among others. In fact, they were the primary supplier of animal traps to the Hudson Bay Company. They began the manufacture of silverware in 1877 and it is the sole remaining industry. There's a good chance your set of 'good silverware' comes from the current incarnation of this industry.

They had a communal dwelling house, they appointed administrative committees and set up a pattern of living that lasted for 30 years. One of the more unique qualities of this community was that the women had equal status to the men in religious and administrative duties and responsibilities and shared in all activities. This is a huge split from previous polygamous arrangements in which women were most often considered property of the men. There was a communal childcare system in place so both men and women could work, and the females adopted a style of dress that consisted of a short skirt over trousers that afforded them greater freedom of movement than contemporary styles.

Starting in 1849, several smaller branches of this group arose around New York state and by 1878 there were 306 members total from all the communities combined.

The breakup started when Noyes began to hand over leadership to his son, who was agnostic and ran the community with 'a tight fist' that the members resented. Noyes came back to lead, but the factions within the community resulting from the poor leadership of his son combined with pressure from surrounding communities caused Noyes to abandon the Complex Marriage concept. The members were too accustomed to the Complex Marriage arrangement and could not settle down to 'normal life'. In January 1881 they reorganized themselves and created a joint-stock company called the

Oneida Community Limited and the Oneida Community was abandoned. More on the Oneida Community.

On March 21st, 1851, Josiah Warren and Stephen Pearl Andrews started Modern Times, an individualist anarchist colony in Long Island, NY. It was based on the idea of 'individual sovereignty' and 'individual responsibility'. All individuals were to pursue their own interests as they wanted to, and all products of labor were private property. They had their own private currency that they exchanged for trade goods and labor. There was no system of authority, no courts, jails or police, and there were also no reports of problems with crime.

Polyamory and polygamy were not specifically part of the tenants of this community, but rather a total lack of 'what should be', which included the right to live non-monogamously if one sees fit. It is believed that the Civil War is one of the most contributing factors in the groups dissolution. Warran abandoned the project in 1862. In 1864, its name was changed to Brentwood, NY.

The extreme repression of the Victorian era found its release in a massive rise in prostitution and pornography. There were a reported 50,000 prostitutes in London and over 300,000 copies of the book A Monk's Awful Disclosures sold before the Civil War.

With the Industrial Revolution in America at the 20th Century, families lost ties with extended relatives and neighbors as close emotional confidantes, and husbands and wives were required to meet their needs for intimacy completely within the context of marriage and their spouse. Society began to reject the emotional claims of friends and relatives, seeing them as competition for spouses with regards to time and attention. The 1950s saw this social concept reach its height in which women were expected to find total fulfillment in marriage and motherhood only.

But with the war effort in the 1960s, women had to leave the home and rediscovered the joys of social contacts and friendships outside of their husbands. A very deep schism has appeared in American society of those who maintain that their spouse should be able to fulfill all emotional and physical needs and those who recognize that humans are social and sexual beings and that one person cannot possibly fulfill every single need for their partner. Stephanie Coontz writes about the decline in social connections and the rise in dependency on a single person (the spouse) to supply all of one's emotional needs.

A researcher who worked with the Cheyenne Indians in the 1930s and 1940s told the story of a chief who wanted to get rid of two of his three wives. The wives joined ranks and said that if he sent two away, he would have to send the third as well.

It wasn't until the rise of the Industrial Age, post the Victorian Era, that it became acceptable to marry for love. Suddenly, love was the only reason that marriage was acceptable. Up until this time, the idea that a marriage should include love was not only thought to be unimportant, it was strongly advised against, claiming that loving one's spouse was dangerous and took away from the love and duty one should hold for God and one's extended family.

The belief that tenderness and excitement of love could coexist with household cares and childrearing brought about the 'traditional marriage' concept currently being debated in the U.S. and other Western countries. The rising divorce rate was not a sign of a lack of values, but rather a consequence of believing that a marriage should include love, as more and more people refused to settle for loveless marriages or marriages where the love is no longer. The Industrial Revolution made this even more possible by giving women economic power of their own, and consequently, the ability and freedom to leave unhappy marriages.

'Dating' evolved in the 1920s as a new way of mate selection. Many conditions of romantic relationships after the Victorian Era were very similar to Roman times, in that women had economic and legal emancipation, children became a luxury rather than an asset, and sexual enjoyment was seen as a 'right'. The main difference was that the Romans moved away from marriage while Americans became more marriage-minded than ever.

China allowed polygamous marriages until the Marriage Act of 1953 after the Communist Revolution.

From 1960-1980, the Ethnographic Atlas Codebook derived from George P. Murdock's Ethnographic Atlas recorded the marital composition of 1231 societies. Of these societies, 186 societies were monogamous. 453

had occasional polygyny, 588 had more frequent polygyny, and 4 had polyandry. That's right ... 85% of the world's population included some form of polygamy. Because of the considerable resources required to support multiple wives, polygynous societies often depict multiple wives as a status symbol denoting wealth and power.

In 1961, author Robert Heinlein wrote a book called 'Stranger In A Strange Land' that emphasized open sexual relationships and used such terms as 'Line Marriage' and 'Nesting' and is arguably the most referenced work of fiction depicting plural partnerships. He wrote several other books that dealt with this topic, including 'Time Enough For Love'.

In 1969-1976, John and Barbara Williamson opened the Sandstone Retreat. It was primarily a nudist-spa type of retreat where a small group of nudist/swingers lived year round in a communal sort of intentional community and on weekends, adults over 18 could join as members and enjoy leisure and health-sponsored activities, full nudity indoors and outdoors, large buffet-style dinners and, in the upstairs 'Ballroom', members could, if desired, engage in swinging and group sex. The founders of Sandstone held some ideas that will be very familiar to poly folk. John and Barbara believed in personal growth through relationships and openness and honesty as the cornerstone to healthy relationships and healthy individuals.

They encouraged communal living and do-it-yourself therapy sessions to remove jealousy and possession from relationships. John and Barbara were very egalitarian, believing that women should be equal contributors to the relationship and to society, even when that meant a woman taking on a traditionally male role, if that's what made her happy. John and Barbara Williamson believed their views of love, respect, and lack of privacy would transform the world. Their work centered around getting existing married couples to open their relationship to sexual and intimate encounters with other people, to eradicate jealousy, and to grow, emotionally, as an individual.

In 1970, the Los Angeles Public Welfare Commission denied the Sandstone Retreat a 'growth center' license which prompted a lengthy and expensive court battle, forcing the Williamsons to sell the club. An appeals court eventually overturned the decision and Sandstone reopened in 1974 under the management of Paul Paige, a former US Marine and marriage counselor. Paul shared the Williamson's idealistic views, but was more pragmatic about money. He instituted annual dues of $740.

The story of the Sandstone Retreat was later mentioned in several books and articles about the sexual revolution, including Esquire, Playboy, Penthouse, The Los Angeles Times, The Sandstone Experience by Tom Hatfield, Thy Neighbor's Wife by Gay Talese, Oui magazine, and Barbara Williamson even appeared on The Dick Cavett Show. They also boasted such famous members as the above-mentioned authors, Dr. Alex Comfort (author of

The Joy Of Sex, which also mentioned the Sandstone Retreat and lyricist for Pete Seeger), journalist Max Lerner, Bernie Casey (a football star and actor), Daniel Ellsberg (famous government critic).

1971-1991 saw the creation of the Kerista Commune, an intentional community centered in San Francisco, CA that was essentially started by Brother Jud Presmont. They were made up of several smaller family clusters of between 4 and 15 people each who were sexually fidelitous to each other. They had a work-optional lifestyle and shared income. They also had a free newspaper and several magazines that discussed their philosophies, and they became one of the biggest Apple computer resellers when the computer industry was revolutionized by IBM competitors. At its height, Kerista had 33 members in several locations.

The group eventually broke up when their unofficial leader, Jud, left and the group could not maintain itself without his leadership. One of the contributing factors, given by another founding member, Eve Furchgott, was that the sense of communism within the group created a lack of personal motivation and individuality that eventually caused disgust in several members because the living spaces were rarely kept clean and household finances were 'in the red for years'.

In the 1970s, Geo of the Kerista Commune created the word 'polyfidelity', which means faithful to many. It is generally reserved for a sexually fidelitous group marriage of co-equals - all equally bonded to each other member.

In 1990, Debora Anapol used the phrases 'non-monogamy' and 'intimate networks'. She was also one of the first authors to use the term 'polyamory' in print, a couple of years later. Also in 1990, Morning Glory Zell, who is actually attributed for coining that term, published an article called 'A Bouquet of Lovers' in her church magazine Green Egg, in which she used the term 'poly-amorous'. It is reported that Morning Glory Zell-Ravenheart and her spouse Oberon Ravenheart discussed the semantics dilemma of not having an inclusive term that encompassed all forms of multiple-love/sex relationships during the process of writing that article and came up with the Latin and Greek combination of 'poly-amory'.

In 1999, the Oxford English Dictionary contacted Morning Glory and requested an official definition for the word 'polyamory'. She took the opportunity to explain that 'polyamory' is meant to mean all forms of multiple loving relationships but is not meant to include multiple purely-sexual relationships like swinging and casual sex.

As of 2006, Indian marriage laws are dependent upon the religion of the people involved. Hindu marriage laws specifically prohibit polygamy for Hindu, Jains, and Sikhs. However, Muslims in India are allowed to have multiple wives.

'In some societies, traditional marriage meant one woman wedded to several men. In others, a woman could take another woman as a 'female husband.' In China and the Sudan, when two sets of parents wanted to forge closer family ties and no live spouse was available, one set sometimes married off a child to the 'ghost' of a dead son or daughter of the other family. Among the Bella Coola and Kwakiutl native societies of the Pacific Northwest, two families who wished to become in-laws but didn't have two sets of marriageable children available for a match might even draw up a marriage contract between a son or daughter and a dog belonging to the desired in-laws. Most traditional marriages were concerned with property and wealth, not love or sex. (taken from Stephanie Coontz)

Throughout history, marriage has been mainly used as a method to control property. Love and sex have been seen as separate from marriage, except where paternity affected property laws. People, as a group, have never successfully maintained sexually monogamous relationships. Even societies that consider themselves monogamous show a high incidence of 'cheating' or secret multiple sexual partners.

Current American society values monogamy highly, but most people participate in either cheating or serial monogamy (or both), suggesting that humans do not necessarily remain monogamous with only one partner for life, even when they claim to want to.

Chapter Three

Reasons Why Polyamory Does Work

Polyamory instigates social stability. After the Crusades many men had died and women were often left alone without any support and without means of survival. Men took it upon themselves to marry numerous women to rebuild communities and reduce poverty. While the context has changed dramatically over the last five hundred years, the Middle East is still rife with internal conflict and there are comparatively far too many women for the society to support without the practice of polygamy helping them gain financial support for their children and for their education.

Polyamory is the answer to unfaithful marriages. Christianity does not endorse cheating, but in countries such as the UK, USA, and Australia, where Christianity is the most prevalent religion, 50-60% of married citizens claim to have indulged in extra-marital affairs. Polyamory keeps sex within the family home and while the women in these marriages can not look to sex outside of their relationship with their husband, everyone can rest assured (to a greater extent) that sex is transparent within this relationship. Your husband is accountable to every one of his wives and you will know where he is every night of the week! Bonus! (Working hours for professionals in the Gulf states are usually significantly shorter than those in New York, London, and

Sydney, so secretarial-fetishism is virtually non-existent; this means no pseudo 'late business meetings' etc).

Polyamory emphasises equal recognition of women. A man is not allowed to found a polyamorous family and must remain monogamous unless he can be completely scrupulous with the equal division of time, resources, money, and education between each of his wives and their families. A man can possess even the tiniest preference for one of his potential wives. If he spends two nights with one wife, then he must spend two nights with the others to balance out the equation. This form of equality is normally breached in modern Western relationships.

Typically, when someone divorces and remarries they pay little or no attention to the previous partner. Women and their children often fall below the poverty line after divorce. Also, men such as Bill Clinton buy nicer presents for their mistresses or have more sex with their mistresses – hardly any equality for poor Hillary. Islamic women have always had the right to divorce, and during separation the husband must still pay maintenance for his ex-wife and children. Catholic women have never had to the right to divorce, so on this front Islamic women really do experience greater freedoms.

Polyamory makes more biological sense than monogamy and polyandry. Zealous feminists (or men who have a lot of respect for women... bless their hearts) may ask why women shouldn't attempt to secure more than one husband if the opposite is morally viable. I myself pondered this question, but when it comes to procreation women's health is of critical importance for 9 month sessions at a time, and a long cue would form for men to impregnate the female in question (apologies for making procreation sound so mechanical and sterile).

Basically, through morning sickness, back pain, and other pregnancy-related conditions, the female can not sustain the work that four husbands require (sustaining the needs of one would surely be difficult enough). This reality impedes upon point 3, which is the basis of polyamory.

Polyamory is undeniably healthier for you! STDs are not rampant in the Middle East, statistics show this, particularly compared to Western nations or southern African nation states. Because all sexual acts are effectively supposed to take place within the confines of marriage, the risk of disease occurring and spreading from social group to social group is almost decimated. While this can't work in practice 100 % of the time, the structure of polyamory has proved over the centuries to be an excellent form of health harm minimization.

Polyamory creates a support network for women and their children. In the West, as a result of working parents, children often have to go to daycare and grow up being taught by individuals outside of the family. Mum and Dad work full-time, they are exhausted when they return home after 10 to 12 hours on the job , they collapse in front of the t.v. and watch the Biggest Loser, then they check their emails and go to bed. Arab culture places a heightened emphasis on the family as an institution and praises women as the focal point of the family sphere.

Polygamy makes men a part of every aspect of the pregnancy process but acknowledges that there are just some things that men can not comprehend, and thus provides extra support with the wives coming together and helping each other when each wife is pregnant or trying to deal with each individual child. Women are never left to bring up a child on their own, a reality which is a strong part of Western culture.

Big families can still exist. It is widely acknowledged that Italy now has the lowest birth rate in Europe; why are the Catholics letting down their Pope?? In the UK, USA, and Australia, we have similarly seen the advent of the one child family, a phenomenon that leads to an empty house, a lack of cousins, a boring family atmosphere. No bullying, no competitive backyard cricket matches, no dressing your little brother up in feminine apparel. There is already unfounded speculation that Arabs will outbreed Western nations in the next 20 years (shame on the media and certain politicians for making contraception a racial issue) because, in my opinion, the minority groups have got their priorities right - families matter. Children matter.

For society to function over a long period of time and replenish itself from generation to generation there is no way of getting around the fact that we need to have children; and polyamory is the answer to lower birth rates in the West.

Men must take responsibility for their actions. There are plenty of men out there who are irresponsible with their relationships, their sex lives, and their semen. Under the model of polyamory, this is not the case. There are hundreds of thousands of men out there in Europe and the Americas who have fathered children and yet don't pay child support or refuse to recognize that the child is their own. Within polyamory, it is imperative that each woman a man has sex with, he must commit to on a spiritual level, an emotional level, a contractual level, and a financial level.

Unlike in the West where men can amass a sexual record upwards of fifty or one hundred names (or... no names in the case of drunken one-nighters) without any repercussions, sense of guilt, or form of connection to these women (such as Hugh Hefner who claims he has slept with upwards of 2000 women, and has the footage to prove it), polyamory stresses maturity and integrity in the choice of partners. Polyamory places emphasis on making the right choice when it comes to a companion, instead of sampling hundreds of partners and not giving proper recognition to women.

To be realistic, the average Western man in his lifetime has at least eight more sexual partners than the average Western woman, so the sex ratio is radically reduced in the case of - for example - one man and four wives. People often state that the social structure of polyamory is solely for the man to exercise the role of sexual stud, perusing the streets for his many lusty virgins. This is simply not true.

Women can have a brilliant career, and bring up well-adjusted children. Not every woman feels like preparing dinner for the family after a long day at work. If one wife in a polyamorous house is working more than the others, another wife will decide to take care of her children during the day and will cook for all of the families at night. Most Western families expect working mothers to do everything; work, then cook, clean, pack kids lunches, make dinner, and fit in board meetings and business trips too. Polyamorous marriages are more flexible for women and their time, as there is the knowledge that the house will always be clean, the children will always be fed and cared for. No need for expensive nannies. No need to feel guilty when you go back to work after you give birth, or get a promotion.

Polyamory forces disrespectful jerks to reform. In a polyamorous society, since there are more single men (because there are less women available) there is more competition between males to win the affection of females. This means that guys have no choice but to work on their charisma, they have to fine-tune their treatment of women, and they have to work harder to establish good reputations in their careers and in their communities. This means that arrogant idiots or men with aggression problems in society are left out in the cold; forcing men to yield to values that will earn them status among women. The message is clear and precise: If you refuse to respect the importance of women and treat them with the care and consideration they deserve, you will die a cold lonely death.

Now how can we implement this in our own culture?

Chapter Four

How to Transition From Monogamy to Polyamory

Polyamory, the practice of having multiple love relationships concurrently, and with the knowledge and consent of everyone involved, has been getting a lot of media attention in the last couple of years. Many married and traditionally monogamous people are now interested in knowing if polyamory may be something they and their spouse can try. But before you and your spouse dive into finding other lovers, and other relationships, there are a few things you may want to think about.

Polyamory is not for the faint of heart. It is not for people who are fearful and skittish, because experimenting with opening your monogamous relationship to other loves will likely bring to the surface some of your most deep seated insecurities. You can communicate and work through them, but it will almost surely be painful and difficult and if you aren't ready to face some tough issues, then now is probably not the right time for you to try polyamory.

Polyamory is not medicine for a troubled relationship. If your relationship is rocky already, it is probably not a great time to try opening it up and involving other people. The monogamy to polyamory transition works best when it is started from a stable, strong relationship.

Both you and your partner should be on the same page about wanting to try polyamory. If one person is pressuring the other to open the relationship and the other person really wants to remain monogamous, then there is likely to be tension and possibly even resentment surrounding the idea of trying polyamory. Successful polyamorous relationships work when both partners want to be polyamorous. While there are poly-mono relationships, ones where only one person is poly and the other is monogamous, these special pairings come with their own set of challenges to cope with.

Honest communication is key in any polyamorous relationship and is particularly critical in the first stages of transitioning from monogamy to polyamory. It is important for each partner to state clearly their desires, expectations and fears and for the other partner to listen non-judgmentally and compassionately. During the transition, keeping the lines of communication open by checking in often with your partner will likely make the foray into polyamory much smoother. People often say that their communication skills improve from discussing polyamory with their partners.

Polyamory certainly is a topic about which many people have very strong opinions and emotions, but by following these guidelines, you too can make the transition from monogamy to polyamory and successfully incorporate other loves into your relationship.

Polyamory and the Penis

With a more-open dialogue about sex and relationships, more and more people are jumping on the polyamorous bandwagon. While it's currently estimated that five percent or less of the people in the United States are living a polyamorous lifestyle, that number is on the rise as only half of millennials are looking for a completely monogamous relationship. While people consider managing emotions as one of the issues to keep a close watch on, men should also be focused on what polyamory means for their penis.

Let's unpack polyamory, how it can affect the penis, and ways to keep the penis in good form if polyamory is for you.

Stigma of Polyamorous Relationships

In American culture, relationships, commitment, and sex are synonymous with monogamy. However, this is not always the case. Monogamy is defined by Merriam-Webster as 'the state or practice of being married to only one person at a time' or 'of having only one sexual partner during a period of time.' Alternatively, polyamory is defined as 'the state or practice of having more than one open romantic relationship at a time.'

The word polyamory derives from both Greek (poly) and Latin (amory) roots and can be directly translated to mean 'many loves.' This is an idea of which popularity has risen a great deal in mainstream media over the last couple of decades.

To the average American, monogamy represents a normal part of life. Children grow up dreaming of finding their one-true love or soul-mate, objectives which are heavily emphasized in many popular television shows and film. People who choose a non-monogamous lifestyle are often considered to be violating important social norms. Because monogamy has been weaved into American society over the course of years, there are many factors aiding its persistence in the community.

All 50 states in the U.S. have standing laws prohibiting polygamy and nearly half of them have statutes against adultery. The relevance in these laws is that a couple who is married in those states cannot legally be involved in polyamorous relationships, even if those relationships are mutually agreed upon. This increases the likelihood of dissonance occurring between partners in a polyamorous setting.

Religious beliefs, moral edicts, and opinions held by the general public are a few other factors working in favor of monogamy. The concept of polyamory is one which often holds negative connotations among the populace. Many people have moral or religious obligations which hold them back from accepting more liberal approaches to love and relationships. This is important to note because it demonstrates why people may be hesitant in joining a polyamorous community or transitioning into an open relationship.

In general, people tend to view monogamous relationships in a more positive light than polyamorous relationships. The overall consensus held by the general public is that couples in non-monogamous relationships are not happy. One possible reason for this may be that the idea of polyamory threatens the cultural image of what marriage should look like and upsets the status quo. These are only a few of the social hardships couples may face by choosing a polyamorous lifestyle over a monogamous one.

Polyamorous relationships are built on a foundation of open and honest communication among all partners. It has often been emphasized in research that poly love involves hard work along with a dedication to each partner. Polyamory, like monogamy, is rooted in love. This love may be expressed emotionally, spiritually, sexually, or all three. Several researchers have stressed that poly love is based on the values of freedom, honesty, and commitment. This is relevant because it gives a new perspective on how non-monogamous relationships can be arranged. The tendencies to rely on deceit or lies to cover up infidelity are no longer an issue. However, other issues can arise involving the communication between partners. One issue that is often a point of contempt for many people is jealousy.

People often assume that polyamorous relationships are synonymous with feelings of jealousy and betrayal that often rise with the knowledge of their spouse or partner engaging their needs with another lover. However, this is not necessarily a bad thing. Polyamorous relationships open the door for an individual's needs to be met by several partners, which takes the pressure off one romantic partner to meet overset expectations. Some researchers even employ the notion that polyamorous relationships may satisfy a person's sexual and emotional needs to a greater degree than do monogamous relationships.

These ideas support the indication that change does occur involving the communication between newly polyamorous couples. However, change is not always a bad thing and may possibly even work to strengthen the honesty and commitment between significant others.

Why Monogamy is Unnatural & Responsible Non-Monogamy Can Save a Relationship

It's difficult for many of us to see how responsible non-monogamy can save a relationship; fears and misconceptions about this emotionally touchy subject can interfere with understanding how it can be beneficial. Although non-monogamy is not for everyone and is not always appropriate, below is a comparison of monogamy and responsible non-monogamy. Note: cheating, lying, unsafe sex, and promiscuity are not part of responsible non-monogamy. Complete and radical honesty with your partner is, and that seems to be what's most threatening and challenging to many of us.

With the custom of monogamy, you own each other, sort of like how you own property. Your partner is yours and if they even look at someone else the wrong way anger and jealousy are common.

With responsible non-monogamy, a couple accepts that owning the rights to each other isn't love, but possessiveness. What about the possibility of one of them falling in love with someone else and abandoning the other? This can happen in any relationship because you don't need to sleep with someone to fall in love with them. Furthermore, it seems that when two people are destined to meet and fall in love they will, regardless of whether or not they are single or involved.

With the custom of a traditional commitment and monogamy, falling in love with someone means that fantasies (such as 'together forever' and 'you are mine for the rest of my life' and 'grow old together') become expectations, and when they aren't met it results in disappointment, heartache, anger, and even divorce.

A responsibly non-monogamous couple tends to accept their relationship as it is rather than how they want it to be or how it's 'supposed to be.' They realize that if their relationship fades or their partner falls in love with someone else, that's the way it was likely destined to be. If your relationship ends, wouldn't you rather accept that there is a more appropriate match out there instead of pretending that your existing connection is 'the one' forever?

With the custom of monogamy, when someone cheats it is kept secret. Because monogamy and honesty are often assumed in relationships, both the cheater and the person being cheated on are at risk for contracting STDs. According to statistics, over 50% of men and women in 'committed' relationships cheat on their partners. Is assumed monogamy realistic or safe?

With responsible non-monogamy, because there are no sexual secrets, a couple is more likely to discuss and practice safe sex.

With the custom of monogamy, based on the above statistics, the illusion of monogamy is much more important to many people than honesty.

Responsibly non-monogamous couples, on the other hand, place more value on radical honesty because truthfulness brings them closer together. In light of this, responsible non-monogamy could potentially reduce the divorce rate and introduce a deeper level of honesty in relationships.

With the custom of monogamy, it's common to blame an ex-partner and their affair for the reason why the relationship didn't last. It's interesting to note that the policy of strict monogamy is never blamed in these situations, yet many who cheat appear better suited for non-monogamy. Truth be told, some people (both men and women) feel like caged animals in long-term monogamous relationships.

With the custom of monogamy, the topic of exclusive intimacy often is not discussed, but is usually expected. Is this always realistic or even reasonable, especially when you know the person has strayed in previous relationships or sense he or she isn't the kind of person who would be happy being sexually exclusive with one person for the rest of his or her life?

That brings us to related topics: *Can we honestly expect sexual passion to last decades in all relationships?* Also, what happens if one partner loses interest in sex or if one reveals, years later, that he or she really doesn't like sex and wants to avoid it? Masturbation is not a good long-term substitute for sexual intimacy.

With the custom of monogamy, you are supposed to be attracted to your partner and only your partner. If you have desires for or fantasies about someone else, even if you don't act on them, they are kept secret. This form of dishonesty can drive a wedge between couples.

With responsible non-monogamy, the couple acknowledges that we are all human and an attraction to someone else, especially during a long-term monogamous relationship, is natural.

A responsibly non-monogamous couple puts their commitment to each other and their relationship first so an attraction to someone else is less of a threat. It is natural to feel insecure or jealous if your partner is attracted to someone else, and it's going to happen whether you're monogamous or not, but when a couple is open and honest with each other about the subject it's a lot less likely to cause a problem.

What about children, you ask? Some responsibly non-monogamous and progressive couples create a 'commitment contract,' where financial arrangements and planning covering possible scenarios (together for 5 years, 10 years, 20 years, etc.) are agreed upon prior to marriage and before children are conceived. A new concept? Hardly. Ancient Egyptians had 5 and 10 year marriage contracts. If mutually agreed upon, they would renew. Although it's not easy to address the subject like you would a business matter, it's much tougher to do so later in divorce court. If two people are unwilling to confront or unable to agree on these issues before marriage it's a red flag for their longevity as a couple.

With the custom of monogamy, sex is love, and if your partner has sex with someone else, they've betrayed you emotionally and it must mean they don't love you anymore.

Responsibly non-monogamous couples realize that while love can be expressed through sex, sex in itself with a secondary partner (if okay with all involved--including the primary partner) does not have to diminish the love already established with the primary partner, nor does it put the primary relationship at risk, if the primary connection is solid. Something real cannot be threatened. This idea is similar to having one best friend and many good friends; you don't expect your best friend to fulfill everything for you that many friends do.

With the custom of monogamy, often it's 'No cheating or else!'

Responsibly non-monogamous couples realize that giving such an ultimatum is about as effective as telling your teenager never to drink alcohol. It's more effective to discuss the issue and to have a 'no punishment policy' for your kids if they call you for a ride to avoid driving drunk or to avoid riding with someone who is drinking and driving. Similarly, such a policy for responsible non-monogamy will encourage honesty and can strengthen the commitment.

Lastly and most importantly, if we cheat, even if no one finds out, negative karma is incurred and we set ourselves up for a similar situation to 'happen to' us in the future. Whatever action we take will, in time, come back to us, so even though radical honesty in relationships may be difficult it is often the best policy. The eyes of truth are always watching us.

Monogamy and Infidelity

Infidelity occurs when a married person engages in a relationship with another person, violating the sanctity of marriage. Infidelity often does not come overnight or by accident - it usually takes place over a period of time, when experiences shared with the new person become more meaningful compared to experiences with a marriage partner. Infidelity can occur without sex coming into the picture.

According to studies, those who commit infidelity go through two stages. First, they consciously decide to seek fulfillment with someone else other than their husband or wife. They then go on to engage in 'acts of infidelity' in secret - but these acts need not be sexual. Whenever a person gives to a new partner outside the marriage what was previously reserved for his or her spouse (be it time, money, confidences, intimacies and other experiences), they are being unfaithful.

Men and women view extramarital affairs in distinctly different ways. Women are usually drawn into adulterous relationships emotionally, while men go about it using their sexual instincts.

It is interesting to note that both tend to assume that the other is acting out of the same motivation. Women may assume that her husband is emotionally attached to another partner, even when his attraction is primarily physical. Men on the other hand, think that the wife's reaction to another man is safe, as long as she does not show any physical attraction.

Infidelity is most often destructive and fatal to any marriage. Healing from infidelity requires that the betrayed spouse recover first from the trauma of the deception. Recovery from trauma requires tremendous support both from professionals and from loved ones. There is hope for marriages to survive infidelity if the couple is willing to work together to preserve their marital vows. In order for a marriage to survive after infidelity, the involved spouse must recognize the wrongness of his or her illicit affair and should be willing to stop it.

Couples seeking sexual expression beyond the limits of traditional marriage are discovering more venues than ever to explore their wild side. Many have come to the realization that once observed, the standard relationship model that we were all raised to accept as singular truth hasn't served us very well. The monogamy myth has been openly brought into question. Frankly, it's astounding that it took this long.

For years married couples have been conflicted between the acknowledged, monogamous marital standard and their natural inclinations. The short-lived euphoria couples experience throughout their courtship, and on their wedding day more often than not succumbs to the inevitability of infidelity. While many believe at the time that they will be able to endure a lifetime of monogamy, the unfortunate reality is most people are simply not meant to be so. Over time, the pattern has been that the frustration over denying one's impulses will surely seek expression elsewhere. The abysmal divorce rate, in addition to the emotional dissociation that many couples endure throughout wedlock is evidence of this.

Certainly it's easy to see how this condition came to exist. Much of American culture is built around the monogamy standard, if not the ideal that love will conquer all. Certainly our mainstream media, be it television, movies, LiteFM or daytime talk is saturated with romantic notions of two people getting married, and living happily ever after. It rarely happens. The reality is that the nature of relationships, and moreover, conjugal sex has become a punch line in America. Despite the astigmatic presumptions many people make before they wed, they soon discover that a lifetime existing with only one set of shared genetalia is not all that it was cracked up to be. Sex with your spouse tends to be fantastic...for the first few months. After that, well there is always cable TV and Internet porn. Many seek their vicarious thrills elsewhere. *Hardy har har.*

To make matters worse, the fear of having to suffer the judgmental indignation of sex-o-phobic conservatives who would impose an antiquated set of marital values has frequently kept married couples from resolving this conflict. The dread of communicating one's desires to their spouse because they fear a self-help inspired moral reprisal has commonly prevented candor about sexuality. This inherent inner conflict between sexual perception and reality has helped create some stifled, hate filled married folks walking around our suburban malls. Many express the frustration over not orgasming as they have always envisioned through sanctimonious wrath.

Many Americans, who have become angry over their inability to maintain an emotional connection with their spouse, let alone acknowledge their own failures at intimacy, ignore the reality of what's in front of them and focus their negative energies on those who practice a different marital standard than they do. When couples who engage in secular lifestyles are 'outed' to their friends and neighbors, they have often been met with scorn and ridicule.

Many have been released from their jobs, or become social outcasts, and have been forced to relocate their residences. The commonly held belief is that people should engage in traditional monogamy, without using any whips, chains leather, toys, or rubber shrink tubing and major household appliances. Any variation from that standard is to be considered socially deviant...regardless of the results.

Oddly enough, mainstream society seems to apply a different moral standard to couples who DO NOT practice negotiated non-monogamy, yet stray outside the confines of their relationship both physically and emotionally. It would seem that marital indiscretion is more easily forgiven, if not tolerated provided that one makes an attempt at a pretense of monogamy. Couples who mediate their extra marital copulation rarely experience the same level of altruism, rather they must often suffer the inequity of those who perceive themselves as being the bearers of a moral standard that amounts to nothing more than a falsehood accepted without question as conventional wisdom. This is due to generations of conditioning. The hypocrisy of this dynamic is staggering, and further proves that the motivation behind those who would denounce people leading secular lifestyles is hardly about the morality they claim it is. Rather it would appear more that misery loves company.

Women in particular have been made to suffer the indignity of self-righteous sex-o-phobes due to the moral double standard that still exists in this country. As in other countries, many of which cannot boast the human rights standards that we claim here in the United States, women have been made to bear the burden of guilt for sexuality. When an empowered woman chooses to engage in conjugation however frequently, and in whatever manner she desires, mainstream Americana will brand her as a 'slut', or a whore. There is no male equivalent for that. Often those doing the labeling are other women expressing petty jealousy over their own unfulfilling sex lives under the guise of moral righteousness.

Some people are fighting back against this insanity though, and many have become more inclined to openly express their proclivities, rather than capitulate to the angst of the orgasm-less masses. Having had enough of apologizing to holier than thou suburbanites devoted to a matrimonial standard that rarely works, and to the intolerant proletariat who would attack any lifestyle than dares fall outside of their myopic comfort zones, many in secular lifestyles have chosen to stand up and proudly proclaim their kink. Many more, and in particular, those who engage in negotiated non monogamy have come to acknowledge that women should have the same liberty to express their libidos as men, and in doing so, they are more easily accepting of possibilities they have yet to explore.

This is what makes this rebirth of sexuality among people in committed relationships all the more vital to the state of mental health of married people everywhere. It would seem that for many, sensibility is winning out over blind devotion. People have begun questioning conventional wisdom in order to avoid compromising their lives. They are becoming less likely to remain in a marital purgatory; rather they are beginning to seek what other options are out there. Many have come to realize that marriage shouldn't mean the end of sex, or even the type of adult oriented fun that they shared before taking their vows. No longer are married couples so easily willing to settle for the vapid co-habitation their parents endured. These are regular married couples, many of which have children and mortgages but who are beginning to explore aspects of their sexuality that would have been unthinkable just a few years ago.

The city of Las Vegas might consider its main commodity to be gambling, but make no mistake...people go there in the numbers they do because it is the one place in the country where people can escape their otherwise boring lives and act as they would love to act every day in suburbia, but can't for fear of moralistic reprisal. Millions of people go to Vegas not simply to wager their earnings, but to be in an environment that is conducive to adult expression. In fact, the city even markets itself according to this paradigm... *'What Happens in Vegas, Stays in Vegas'*. It is the one place in the country where people do not have to deny their quintessential selves. They dress suggestively; flirt with intent, and party as long as they can hold out. If you have an ethical problem with cleavage, Vegas might not be the best vacation spot for you.

But as people's frustrations over the conflicted nature of relationships increases, the need to let off steam needs to be brought closer to home. Not everyone in search of escape has the means to get themselves to Nevada.

Almost every major city has now become host to at least one annual event that centers on new and different ways to become intimate, fornicate, or simply get your freak on. Whether it be a Swingers party, a Fetish Ball, or perhaps even a Polyamourous retreat... Schoolteachers, CPA's, and other upright community leaders from across the country frequent these types of events so they can work their mojo, if not to simply release the pressure of their everyday lives. Nowhere is this more evident that at the Exotic Erotic Expo & Ball which occurs annually in San Francisco.

Every year around Halloween time an adult oriented carnival occurring over a weekend and culminating in a huge Saturday night Ball caters to an interesting mixture of lifestyles. Otherwise 'normal' husbands and wives dress in their most provocative (if not outrageous) outfits and are able to party uninhibited until the sun comes up without having to endure the moral scrutiny of their neighbors. Billing itself as 'The World's #1, Wildest Sexiest Party', the Exotic Erotic Ball is the type of event that married, mainstream couples look forward to attending once a year so they can let it all hang out. Literally.

The recent Swingfest convention located on Florida's Atlantic Coast proved to be another terrific pressure valve whereby multitudes of lascivious, sex-positive eroti-philes were able to escape the doldrums of their otherwise circumscribed lives, and explore the boundaries of their libidos. Literally thousands of couples, many of whom were merely curious as to what the limits of their comfort ability might be, chose to attend a weekend soiree' wrought with sex workers, adult film stars, and other average everyday suburban couples whose lifestyle allow them to engage in extra marital fornication. 'I am bringing my husband here for our anniversary,' said a 20-something little hottie named Stacey. 'I am not exactly sure what to expect.'

Neither did anyone else, in fact, as this was the folks at Swingfest's first ever convention. However, not knowing what to expect is the reason so many people are choosing to attend events like this in the first place. Although the immediate association one makes with Swingfest is that it is strictly a swingers convention, the truth is that what made the event overflow from the over 990 room beachfront Westin Diplomat Resort into two neighboring hotels was that it's appeal was to a much larger group of sexual enthusiasts. 'What Swingfest was about was to bring different communities together' said Jason Jean, owner of the event, 'We set out to throw the world's largest Swinger's party, but without excluding other communities'.

The unique feature behind Swingfest seemed to be that nobody was apparently excluded from the adult oriented fun. Provided they weren't there to discuss their crab grass, every attendee seemed to have an outlet to explore whatever it was they were looking to experience, regardless of their experience attending these types of events. Although the core attendees were in fact people who engaged in negotiated non-monogamy, there was a large contingent present that were there to learn, seek out what their prospects were, or even dabble in inter-relationship carnal knowledge for the first time.

In fact, just as with the Exotic Erotic Expo, one doesn't need to have a lifestyle beyond traditional monogamy to be able to enjoy booth surfing at the Swingfest expo. Whether shopping for erotic art, clothing, sex toys, or even having the opportunity to meet industry related entertainers, these adult oriented marketplaces are great ways to initiate couples into a world beyond backyard barbeques and office holiday parties. Walking through a suggestively charged expo floor has a way of heightening one's sense of sexuality. Also for the novice attendee, Swingfest offered several seminars to help along couples that may have either felt overwhelmed, or who just needed a better understanding of specific aspects of secular marital lifestyles.

Even for the veteran swinger there were opportunities to prospect and delve into things that they might have yet to experience. But make no mistake, the allure of Swingfest was the wild parties, and the potential for couples to meet one another and engage in extra marital copulation. During the day the beach and the two more than ample sized pools were more than able to accommodate the massive amount of sexually expressive people who were there mingle with purpose. By the time the nighttime festivities rolled around, those who were there to do what swingers do were a mere elevator ride away from experiencing the excitement of having intercourse with people who they had recently met.

But there is a growing phenomenon that centers on committed couples looking to expand their matrimonial horizon. People are becoming tired of the failures of institutionalized marriage. Perhaps without having the knowledge of what possibilities may be available to them, they do realize this much; the existing plan isn't working.

Chapter Five

The Future of Love and Relationships

Imagine living in a society where everyone was extremely psychic, and also fully embraced the tenets of karma, fate, and reincarnation. What would your love life be like?

What follows is how we perceive things will be in 500 or more years, and also, according to our past life regression empirical research, how relationships were recognized in certain advanced lost civilizations, thousands of years ago.

- **People will see the purpose of each relationship before it begins:**

They'll look back in wonder about how, hundreds of years earlier, relationships were expected to be predominantly about romance and serving personal agendas.

Sure, a little romance can add spice to a relationship, but in the future humanity will be psychic enough to realize that there is a different purpose for every connection, everyone has many soul mates, and not all of those connections are meant to involve lasting harmony and romance.

The karma, both 'good' and 'bad,' with every person you meet, will be obvious, so romantic illusion won't cloud judgment. Instead of hoping that each new possibility is 'the One' (which is too easy to do now because of the influence of movies, TV and pop culture, in general), people will simply sit back, relax, and perceive what is most likely meant to transpire based on what happened between them in past lives and where they left off.

- **Jealousy and possessiveness will cease to exist:** Trying to own or control a partner in any way will be regarded as archaic and dysfunctional. No one will feel a need to because though more people will be single, the relationships that do develop will be so compatible and strong that the thought of someone else coming between them won't be considered a threat.

- **Cheating and lying will be almost non-existent:** Likewise, because everyone will be able to perceive themselves and others honestly, they'll accept that strict, life-long monogamy is not ideal for everyone. Those for whom it isn't, about 50% of the population, will no longer make promises of life-long fidelity and it won't be expected of them either. As a result, responsible non-monogamy and group relationships will be more popular as an alternative to dishonesty.

- **Far fewer will marry:**

Those that do will wait until later in life, and there will be different forms of marriage. Some will choose to have what we now call traditional marriage because of their happy shared lifetimes of the same. Other couples will mirror different relationship models that worked for them in their past lives.

- **People won't feel the need to get married before having kids:**

They'll also accept that marriage does not guarantee happiness and security for a child and since the focus will be more on the child than their relationship, 'child contracts' will be more popular than marriage contracts. These will, among other things, put the child first and protect the child and the primary caretaker of the child.

One of the best things about a high level of psychic ability is the awareness of unlimited love from within and the other side. The romantic love so many seek now pales in comparison with this. People will feel more joyous and complete on their own, which will result in far more healthy and satisfying relationships.

Vision of a New Morality

When looking at society, and seeing the constant hypocrisies, the inconsistencies, the lies, a person can be inclined only towards two mindsets. They will go along with what they see, they will believe what they are told, they will find it awkward that anyone could challenge things the way they are. Or, they will see the outrightly absurd nature of things, they will see the lies, they will see the propaganda, they will see the inconsistency, and they will refuse to believe it. They will cry out for anything but this society -- they will seek out reason, logic, truth. Anything that is well-reasoned will sooth their heart, anything that is logically demonstrated will be at peace with their mind. Their life will be transformed into a journey, ceaselessly looking for the truth, wherever it is, whatever it tells us, no matter what must be sacrificed to discover it.

In our society, we find that there are two people. Those who will accept what they are told, will obey authority, will exist in the way that television and radio has commanded them to exist. And there are those who will condemn the way things are, will resist authority, will point out all the inconsistencies and lies given to us. In generations to come, they will be called heroes. In our own time, they will be called instigators. Historians will regard them as the cause to a change in society. Rationalists will treat them as the finest examples of intelligent people. But what is it that they can truly be called? Searching through the expanse of human language, what name can rightly apply to someone who uses their mind? A person without shackles on their mind, without a blindfold on their eyes, without bondage on their heart, without lies in their mind... may be called a Freethinker.

The theory which may be questioned most by any Freethinker, is the theory of the modern morality. By this, I mean the theory of monogamy, that a person ought to only have one sexual partner at one time. But this theory is more than just that. Not only is it a one-sexual-partner ideal, but it covers other ideas. Those who are promiscuous with their bodies are treated as heartless and brutal. A modern moralist will paint a picture of a slut, and every vice will be given to them. They will say that promiscuous lovers are cruel, are merciless, are vicious, will do anything to get sex, they have no values, they cannot understand love, they are beyond the scope of sympathy... A modern moralist will speak such great lies about the promiscuous lover. Yet, they are wrong. I contend that there is no such thing as a human being who is beyond the scope of sympathy, who cannot understand love. Sympathy and love: these are but the most simple, most basic, most true of all principles to any mammal. I have never known a human being who didn't know the meaning behind tears; I never knew a lover who didn't know the warm touch of affection; even to those who have betrayed me or otherwise believe me to be a vicious mongrel, I know that they too are capable of knowing the truth of love. To say that a promiscuous lover breaks this very basic, scientific rule: the rule that states that all can know love and sympathy is to debauch the face of truth.

The modern moralist will commit more crimes against truth. It is believed that the person who is willing to be physical soonest is of the lowest character, and it is believed that the person holding out the longest is the greatest. A person willing to give a kiss on the face to a person who has been disappointed by life, a person willing to share intimacy and kindness through the physical act of love, a person who knows that being a lover means loving -- this person will be called a 'slut' or a 'whore.' But then, there is another type of person... There will be a man or a woman, who will refuse to touch another from the opposite sex, who will look the other way when someone is attracted to them, who will resist any form of affection.

This person, who has been taught to be revolted at the thought of sex or physical kindness, will be upheld as a saint, as a 'true person of goodness.' These lies that we are told, they sicken me. There was once a time when, with a lover, my fingers caressed the smoothness of her palm, and she kissed my neck. A philosopher who believes in the sanctity of monogamy will look at this, and he will call her a tramp, a slut, a whore. But when I was in the peace of those most cherished moments, I see her angelic face, I feel her soft skin, and in my mind, every trouble is a thousand miles away. For those few brief moments with this lover (who I had known less than an hour), I discovered peace and love. A person who believes in monogamy can speak all they want, they can exhaust the human language as much as they can. But what they say, will never take away the sincerity my lover's affection, will never remove these memories that I tend to revisit when I loss the peace I once had.

What arguments can I offer? What reasoning can I barter with? When I feel the warmth of another's body close to mine, when I know the tender caress on my face... what can I say to defend this lifestyle? Call it 'promiscuity' or 'whoredom,' call it what you like. All the slanders and libels in the world will not detract from the pleasure of it, will not destroy the intimacy of it. When I am looking into the eyes of a lover, I will not be thinking of what they say about me. They will condemn me to hell, but I am deaf to their damnations. They will say I have no virtue, but still, I cannot hear them. So long as my lover is running her fingers through my hair, as my fingertips run down her back, they can say all they want about me, because I am not hearing it. I remember once, as a child, seeing a statue of a man and a woman. The woman was laying back onto the chest of the man, while their hands were met together. It was made by the Etruscan culture. Looking at this statue then, I saw intimacy and kindness. I saw 'I feel I can tell you anything.' I saw 'When I hear you breath, it makes me live.' I saw the gentle emotions of a lover not wishing to cause any distress... In this small Etruscan statue, I found respect, kindness, and truth. It was only several pounds of clay, but it may have contained the secrets of the Universe.

If there is any argument that can be offered on behalf of Free Love, or Polyamory, or whatever name one desires to give the belief that we should not have one sexual partner -- if there is any argument, it is the naturality of sex. Any person who confesses they do not have lust is a liar. And any person who wishes to convince others that their natural lust is immoral, this person is a vagrant.

When the passions that exist between the sexes are natural, when they are a normal part of our minds, when they the act of love is simply a bodily function, on what grounds can it be condemned?

By playing a sport, or by conversating with a friend, or by putting your sincere thoughts on to paper, a person is using the parts of their body. There is nothing wrong with it. There is no crime in it. No one is hurt. But, when a person all of a sudden decides to use their sexual organs, to please their natural desires, to express affection, to know the depths of intimacy, our moralists will call it a crime! By using our body, as we please, for the ends that we desire, and by hurting no one, they call this a crime! But the search for our soul's content, the endless journey of spirituality -- whether it manifests itself in the arms of your lover, or in the books of the ancients -- it has always been condemned by those who were too blind, too ignorant, too set in their ways, to see more than five feet ahead of themselves. The search to know what it means to feel gentle intimacy and friendly kindness, when this search becomes sexual and a person express their desires, the slanders I described above will be put against them.

A man who loves sex will be called a pervert and a woman who hates it will be called a prude. A woman who loves sex will be called a slut and a man who hates it will be called a misguided fool. We are told these lies, over and over, by a society too foolish to think for itself. It has been said by every liberal that freedom means, doing what you will, as long as you do not infringe upon the rights of others. If this is true, if liberty is not a guide but a path to happiness, then by what right can we condemn those who wish to be free form sexual dogma? Why, in fact, deny the natural instincts of one's own sexuality?

When we refuse what our heart seeks out, when we turn away from our desires, when the aching to know the truth that is inside all of us, when it is treated with an anesthetic -- at this point, our soul begins to whither, and our spirit becomes something foreign from when we were first born. If all men are born free, then it is by rejecting our true selves that we become slaves to misery and vice. I do not believe, however, that all men and women seek out sex as the greatest good, nor do I believe they should. I believe that a person should look into their hearts, and see for themselves what they want. They should not be afraid of what society calls them.

They should not be afraid of how their friends react. They should not be afraid of what may happen by discovering their heart's desire. Upon discovering what sex means to them -- whether it is a great means of pleasure, whether it is the most perfect way of expressing one's affections, whether it is a combination of these and other ideas -- once a person discovers what sex means to them, they should live a lifestyle accordingly.

Just take some hypothetical scenarios... If you were alone with a friend whom you cared about deeply, and you knew there was an attraction between you -- and you felt that sex was the greatest way to express your soul -- then what would be so wrong about making such a proposition? Feeling the gentle touch of a lover over your body, there is little more that can be seen as perfect security, as perfect tranquility. What then, would you have gained from such an encounter?

Memories that will serve you in your darkest times, memories of kindness, peace, and intimiacy; physical pleasure; and knowledge. What would be the benefits of refusing such an encounter, when you know that you longed for it in your heart? I can see little. Peace and truth are the greatest ends of every humane person. There should never be a reason for avoiding the path that leads to these humble desires. I had once heard that a person was imprisoned by the government for oral sex, what the law had regarded as a 'Crime Against Nature.' I contend that the greatest crime against nature is refusing what your heart tells you to do, allowing your soul to grow bitter and disenchanted with life.

By this new morality, this idea that it is no crime to rub your face in the neck of your love, to let your fingers speak for your soul... By this new morality, I propose that there should never again be a girl full of tears, because she is lonely but feels sex is immoral. I propose that there should never again be a man frustrated with sex, because his hormones are building up but he feels sex is a crime. I propose that men and women everywhere should throw off the chains of an antiquated morality, of a slavery that kept their heart in bondage. There should never again be a person who compromised the desires of their heart with a vicious society, there should never again be a person who is content with the daemons of loneliness, there should never again be a person who knows the stinging pain of being alone, there should never again be a person doomed to pain -- never again should we allow these tears to amount to nothing, never again should we allow these cries to go unheard -- I propose that every man and woman should not be afraid of sex, that they ought to do as their heart tells them, as long as they make no one suffer...

I propose that our culture adheres closer to the sentiments of kindness and charity, and closer to the principles of truth and reason.

Chapter Six

Jealousy in Relatioships

In my opinion jealousy in relationships is completely misunderstood since we tend to hold extreme positions on the jealousy scale. We either feel that extreme jealousy is justified so that we spend our days in suspicion and mistrust or we feel guilty being jealous when our partner is behaving inappropriately. Obviously therefore there is healthy and unhealthy jealousy in relationships. So what are the attitudes that are central to unhealthy jealousy in relationships?

- **It's basis:**

What is at the heart of your jealousy? Is it part of your baggage from previous relationships or has your partner done something that warrants it? This question can be very hard to answer honestly because you 'view' your partner through the lenses of your hurts and past experiences and thus what you 'see' tends to be distorted. To work out what the root of your jealousy is look at your past and present relationships; do you see a trend? If you see a trend then your jealousy has nothing to do with your partner and is clearly unhealthy.

- **Self value:**

In your heart of hearts do you feel that your partner is your equal or do you think they are too good for you? If you have a sneaky feeling that you are not worthy of your partner then unfounded jealousy will plague you every time you see someone 'more' worthy anywhere near your partner. This is unhealthy jealousy that just sours your relationship. You need to find a way to accept that your partner truly cares for you and not the other 'more' attractive people or you need to find a way to deal with your unfounded jealousy otherwise you will keep sabotaging your relationship.

- **Partner's attitude:**

Do you feel that your partner values you above all else or do you feel that you have to fight for their attention? If you are constantly fighting for your partner's attention then you will tend to be jealous of all the other things that your partner prioritizes over you. This is healthy jealousy but it tends to be misplaced because the problem is your partner and not the other things in their life. You need to get through to your partner that you are unwilling to be last on their priorities.

If they are unwilling to change then you may need to break-up the relationship but if you are unwilling to leave then you must learn to live with the constant jealousy that will be your way of life.

- **Self blame:**

Does your partner behave badly and you feel guilty being jealous or they downplay their bad behavior and make you think that your jealousy is irrational? If this is you then your jealousy is unhealthy in the sense that you are burying your healthy jealousy. Jealousy is an emotion that helps you protect yourself and your relationships and burying it doesn't make it go away. If you genuinely think that your partner's behavior is unacceptable; then follow through with your feelings. You have a right to them and nobody should tell you different.

Jealousy in relationships can be healthy or unhealthy depending on what is driving the jealousy. Healthy jealousy helps you keep boundaries around your relationship and everything else while unhealthy jealousy just keeps you stewing in negativity without doing anything to improve or strengthen your relationship boundaries. In-fact unhealthy relationship jealousy simply erodes your self esteem and gives negativity a stronghold in your relationship.

Handling Jealousy in Relationships

Jealousy in relationships is one of those things that we just can't seem to agree on. Is it bad or good? Some people think it is bad and it should be avoided at all costs while others think that it is good and is a demonstration of how deeply you care for your partner. What do you think; is jealousy in relationships good or bad? When I ponder over it I get the feeling that jealousy is neither bad nor good. It seems to me that it becomes either bad or good depending on the way that you handle it. So what are some key steps in handling jealousy so that it makes your relationship better?

- **Admit it:**

Truth be told, many of us do not want to admit jealousy in relationships as it makes us feel vulnerable. If we admit it to ourselves that we are jealous then doesn't it mean that we care more deeply for our partner then we care to admit? That may be the truth that you don't want to face but it is your truth...face it! Burying it away or pretending that it doesn't exist is a lie and if you suppress it long enough it will come out in inappropriate behavior or speech that is way more embarrassing then if you had simply admitted it to yourself.

- **Analyze it:**

What is your jealousy based on? Is it based on something real or are you just insecure? Sometimes you may be jealous because of all the things that you imagine in your mind or it may be because there is a real reason for the jealousy. Is there a real reason for the jealousy? Think about it so that you can try to separate your insecurities from reality.

To help you sieve out your issues take an honest look into your past relationships...do you see a pattern of jealousy? If there is then the problem may lie with you and not your partner.

- **Deal with it:**

How you do this will of course depend on the basis of your jealousy, the type of relationship that you have and the scale of the jealousy that you feel. If your jealousy is based on your insecurities then you need to find a way to deal with those...and get help if you need it. If on the other hand your jealousy is because your partner's behavior is inappropriate then you need to let them know what specific things in their behavior/attitude bother you. If your relationship is fairly new and you feel a slight pang of jealousy when your partner seems interested in someone else, you may need to find a way to deal with it so that your partner doesn't think your psycho.

Think of ways to let them know in subtle ways what you feel without reading them the riot act. You want them to know what you feel so that they know your relationship barriers. This will help you gauge their level of care for you and if they care and respect you enough to value your relationship barriers. If your partner thinks that you are being silly then your relationship may not have much of a future since what you feel is real to you and your partner should make some effort to make you more comfortable in the relationship.

Jealousy in relationships has a way of sneaking up on many of us but if you follow these 3 steps then you are on your way to dealing with the jealousy and using it to define for you and your partner the relationship barriers that you need to negotiate.

So, how do you handle this jealousy thing?

Nobody is immune to jealousy, of course. It's like being immune to fear or hunger or anger. Some people may be naturally more jealous than others, but anybody can feel jealous. Jealousy, like fear or hunger, is just a feeling.

But jealousy isn't really a response to seeing your partner with someone else, at least not directly. it says more about your own security or insecurity than it does about the actions of your partner.

Jealousy is most common when somebody feels insecure, mistreated, threatened, or vulnerable in a relationship. If you feel secure in a relationship, you don't get jealous. Jealousy is not the problem; jealousy is the symptom of the problem. Address the insecurity or the things underlying the feelings of vulnerability, and you address the jealousy. So the trick to making a poly relationship work is to make everyone involved feel secure, valued, and loved.

A poly relationship depends much more than a traditional relationship on mutual security and trust. Even the smallest amount of insecurity in a poly relationship can quickly be magnified to the point where it can be lethal to the relationship.

The problems are magnified even more if you try not to let your fears and your feelings show. One key to making the relationship work is to talk about your fears, openly and immediately, even if you think they're irrational.

Often, naming your fears, bringing them into the light, deprives them of their power.

I think it's natural to assume that people who aren't monogamous are immune to jealousy, but I don't think it's true. Rather, I think that jealousy is a symptom that something else is wrong. Often, jealousy is a symptom that someone is feeling insecure, or threatened. Address the underlying problem, and the jealousy goes away.

Jealousy, like other emotions, doesn't come from nowhere. It comes from a feeling that someone's needs aren't being met, or someone feels threatened. People who don't feel threatened, don't feel jealous.

The key to defeating jealousy, in my experience, is to address the underlying causes of jealousy—if possible, before they come up. Make your partner feel special, needed, and loved, and your partner will not feel threatened or afraid.

Personally, I'm a big fan of empiricism. One of my favorite quotes is by Francis Bacon, who said, 'Your true self can be known only by systematic experimentation, and controlled only by being known.' I believe that emotions, though they are not rational, do usually have a reason behind them-,-they are the ancient part of your brain, the part that does not have language, trying to communicate with you.

So. The question is, why are you jealous? Jealousy is an unusual emotion, in that it's a feeling that's often built out of other feelings, such as fear or anger or insecurity. What is it that triggers the jealousy, and more important,why? When you think about the things that cause you to feel jealous, what's the first emotional reaction that flashes through your head—fear? Anger? Sadness? Rejection? Loss? What underlies those feelings—fear of losing her? Fear of being insufficient? Anger at someone else moving in on your territory? All of these? None of these?

Since jealousy usually has its roots in some other emotion, such as fear of loss or feelings of rejection or insecurity or whatever, then often the only way to cope with the jealousy is to deal with the underlying emotions. If you find that your jealousy is rooted in fear, for example, the next step is to explore why you are afraid, and what you are afraid of, and if there's anything you can do to allay that fear. Confronting the jealousy head-on without addressing the things that lie beneath it is often an exercise in frustration.

Once you've identified the feelings beneath the jealousy, the next step is to ask yourself: What are these feelings serving? Are they serving a legitimate interest? Are they trying to warn you of a real problem, or are they serving only themselves? This can be very tricky, especially with an emotional response like fear—fear can serve as a legitimate warning of a valid danger, but fear also tends to try to protect itself, and if you're afraid of something with no reason, your fear will try to persuade you that it's valid and you have cause to be afraid.

One thing that's often overlooked, particularly in the poly community, is that there are times when jealousy is a valid and rational response to a situation. If there is a problem in your relationship, or if your partner is using a new relationship as a way to avoid dealing with issues in your relationship, then jealousy is a reasonable response. Separating the jealousy that's a warning of a real problem from the jealousy that isn't is not always an easy task, though.

Where you go from there depends on what you discover about the root of the jealousy. Fear, insecurity, and so forth are all feelings that can be overcome, though usually not without confronting them directly and deliberately exposing yourself to the very things that make you afraid or insecure.

How to build a relationship without jealousy

One of the central fixtures in most polyamorous relationships, especially polyamorous relationships between an existing couple who begin with a monogamous relationship and then expand the relationship to include polyamory, is a set of rules or covenants designed to protect the existing relationship and to make the people in the relationship feel secure—in other words, to deal with issues like jealousy, insecurity, and threat. I'm going to use the metaphor of the refrigerator and bend it to my own ends.

Let's assume your relationship is a refrigerator. One day, a problem arises in your relationship—the refrigerator quits working. You walk into your kitchen, there's a puddle on the floor, and all your frozen pizzas and ice cream are a gooey mass in the bottom of the freezer. There are a few things you can do at this point, once you've mopped up the mess and scraped the remains of last night's lunch out of the fridge. One solution is to fix the refrigerator; another is to replace it. A third solution is to leave the refrigerator exactly where it is and change your life around the problem—'From this day forward, I will bring no frozen or refrigerated foods into this house.' In the poly community, the last option is the one most people choose.

I'll get back to the fridge in a bit, though. First, let me say something important, which is that sometimes, fears have a purpose. I'm going to spend a good deal of the rest of this entry talking about fear and threat, and it's important to keep in mind that not all fear is irrational. Fear of snakes? Positive and healthy. Fear of spiders, or falling, or drowning? Positive and healthy. A lot of our distant ancestors had to die to bequeath us with these instinctual fears, and they've served us well. There's a difference between a rational fear and an irrational fear, a difference between a fear that genuinely keeps you safe and a fear that makes you contort your life (and the lives of the people around you) for no good reason. The latter kind of fear seeks only to protect itself, not to protect you—and ironically, sometimes it creates the very thing you're afraid of!

In a relationship, a fear or an insecurity is a symptom of a problem. In some cases, the fear is perfectly rational and justified. An abused child lives in fear of his abusive parent for good reason; he has tangible reason to fear. In a healthy relationship, though, these fears are almost always irrational and unfounded.

Jealousy itself is an interesting emotion, because jealousy is a composite emotion that is based on other emotions. It's a second-order emotional response—something happens, that thing causes you to feel threatened or to feel insecure or to feel something negative about yourself, and then that fear or insecurity makes you feel jealous. For that reason, the root of jealousy is often surprisingly difficult to pin down and understand.

Instead, what happens is that people look at the event that is the proximal cause of the jealousy and assume that that event is the source of the problem. 'My partner kisses another person, I feel jealous; therefore, it's the kiss that makes me jealous. The way to deal with the jealousy is to tell my partner to stop kissing people.'

Many years ago, I was dating a woman I'd met at college, who I'll call R. During the course of our relationship, R started dating another close friend of mine, T. And for the first time in my life, for the first time in my history (at the time) of a half-dozen successful long-term poly relationships, I was jealous.

I don't mean 'you know, this makes me uncomfortable' jealous. I mean 'completely overwhelmed, smashed to pieces beneath a tidal wave of feelings I could not anticipate or predict or control; gut-wrenching, wanting-to-puke' jealous. I mean the kind of jealous that consumes every other feeling and leaves nothing but ashes behind. I'd never felt those things before, and when I was in the middle of those feelings the only thing—the only thing—I could think about was making the feelings stop, however I could.

Because it happened when she was with T, and didn't happen at other times, I made the logical, reasonable, and totally stupid assumption that the cause of the feelings was her relationship with T. From there, I reached the equally stupid conclusion that the thing that would make the jealousy go away was if she changed something about her behavior or her relationship with T. (I also didn't really recognize the jealousy for what it was, powerful as it was, because I'd never felt it before, which only reinforced the notion that it was 'caused by' her relationship with him.)

I behaved pretty reprehensibly, playing passive-aggressive games and just generally acting like...well, like a lot of people dealing with their first crisis in a poly relationship act. Predictably, it destroyed my relationship with her. She went on to marry T and cut me out of her life completely; the very thing I was afraid of came to pass because of my jealousy. Had I not behaved the way I did, we'd probably still be close, almost 15 years later.

In hindsight, now that I have a lot more experience and a bit more emotional wisdom under my belt, I can see where I went wrong. When a person feels jealous, and attributes the jealousy to the things that trigger the jealousy, he doesn't actually understand the jealousy. It's a bit like a person who has never seen a rabbit except when it's being pursued by a dog believing that the dog is the cause of the rabbit. In reality, jealousy is built of other emotions; jealousy is not 'caused' in any direct sense by the action that triggers it, but rather by a different emotional response to the act that triggers it.

In my case, R and I had never really discussed her relationship with T; nor had we talked about, in any capacity at all, what her intentions with T were or what effect, if any, that would have on her intentions with and her relationship with me. Put most simply, I saw her and T together, I had no idea what that meant for her and me, so I became afraid of being replaced. The fear of being replaced, in turn, led to the jealousy.

Now, had I actually taken the time to examine the jealousy and really try to understand it, I probably would've figured that out. And, once I understood that the jealousy was caused by a fear of being replaced...well, a fear of being replaced is a fear that you can work with. A fear of being replaced, all things considered, is really not that difficult to address. All it requires is conversation about intentions, perhaps a bit of reassurance, and time enough to demonstrate that the conversations and reassurance are genuine, and hey, there you go.

Getting back to the refrigerator:

Fixing the refrigerator means doing exactly that. It means saying, 'I know that I am feeling jealous. I know that the jealousy is brought about by some other emotion—some emotion that is triggered by the action that makes me jealous. I need to figure out what that other emotion is, and I need to figure out why that action triggers that emotion.'

Until you do that, you are helpless in the face of the jealousy. If you don't understand it, there is nothing you can do to address it. Trying to understand it isn't easy; when you're ass-deep in alligators, it's easy to forget that the initial goal was to drain the swamp, and when you're entirely overwhelmed by gut-wrenching emotions that are tearing you to pieces, it's easy to forget that these emotions are grounded in some other emotions. In the middle of jealousy, all you want is for the jealousy to stop, and you don't care how.

So, you confuse the trigger with the cause. You believe, erroneously, that the source of the jealousy is the action that triggers it. You see your partner kiss someone, you feel jealous, you want the jealousy to stop, you pass a rule: 'No more kissing.'

This is the equivalent of saying 'No more frozen food in the house.' The problem is still there. The root has not been touched. The broken refrigerator is still sitting in the corner, dripping water. You haven't actually dealt with the underlying causes at all; you haven't addressed the insecurity or fear of loss or fear of being replaced; you've just 'solved' the problem by shielding yourself from situations that might make you address it. You've 'solved' the broken refrigerator by passing a rule against bringing refrigerated food into the house.

And then you do the same thing to anyone else who comes in to your relationship. You tell anyone coming into the house, 'Look, here's how it is. You can come over, you can have dinner with us, you can spend time here. but under no circumstances are you to bring any frozen food into these premises.' And if anyone asks why—well, secondary partners don't get to ask why, do they? Those are the rules, take 'em or leave 'em. We Just Don't Talk About the giant, leaky, broken refrigerator in the corner. We don't talk about it and we don't allow anything that might make us confront the fact that the damn fridge is busted. No frozen foods. No kissing, no saying 'I love you,' no doing anything that might make us actually have to deal with the refrigerator.

Take it or leave it:

One common situation that arises often among polyamorous people is a fear of competition, or a sense that another person who expresses an interest in your lover is threatening to you. Often, this fear is based on the idea that people who are like you are more threatening than people who are not; as a result, many times people in polyamorous relationships will pass rules like 'I feel threatened if you have another partner who is the same sex as me. You can sleep with other people who are not of the same sex as I am, but do not become involved with people who are the same sex as I am.'

Sometimes it works the other way: 'I don't mind if you have partners of the same sex, because I know what they can offer you and I know I can compete with them, but I get insecure when you have partners of the opposite sex because they can provide an experience I can't.'

Whatever. The emotional process is pretty much the same.

One consequence of a feeling like this (and believe me, this particular feeling is very common—so common it's a cliché) is a couple who will search for that mythical 'Hot Bi Babe' who will sleep with both of them, on the idea that it'll keep anyone from feeling jealous.

In any event, the general idea is this: A person has an existing, primary relationship. One of them, or perhaps both of them, then begin sexual or romantic relationships with others. One of the people in the primary relationship has a jealousy response, such as 'I don't care when you are with a partner of the same sex, but when you are with a partner of the opposite sex I feel insecure.'

Now, put yourself in that position: you are jealous when your partner has some sort of relationship with some other person under some particular circumstance, such as when your partner has sex with someone of the same sex as you. What do you do?

Well, you have a few choices

You can take the 'I'm not the boss of my partner, so I will let my partner do his thing; my jealousy is my issue to deal with, and I shouldn't feel it, so I won't' approach. That usually involves squashing or suppressing the jealousy, which in turn usually means sitting in a dark room crying and feeling like you're going to throw up when your partner is out having fun, sometimes combined with moodiness and passive-aggressiveness when your partner returns...y'know, just to spice things up.

Of course, you're going to feel like crap. Getting back to the refrigerator, this is like continuing to put food into the fridge even though you know it's broken. Result: wilted lettuce and sour milk. Bon appétit!

Or, you can say 'I get jealous if my partner does X or Y with a person of Z sex, so we'll make a rule in our relationship: no X or Y with someone of Z sex.' There you go, you don't feel jealous any more. Of course, the underlying cause is still there—you haven't fixed it. What will likely happen then is that six months down the road, you'll find that action W triggers the same jealousy. Okay, no biggie—we'll outlaw W too. But wait, action Q and S trigger jealousy too—who knew? Hey, we can handle this; we'll pass rules against Q and S. Oh, and against T, too, because T is, y'know, kinda like S. And we'll pass rules against—you know what, this other partner of yours is just making me feel jealous in general. Veto!!!

And then you end up with problems in your own relationship, because, y'know, unintended consequences and all that. One of the unintended consequences of vetoing a person your partner loves is that you hurt your partner; one of the predictable consequences of doing things that hurt your partner is you damage your relationship.

Or, there's a third solution. You can break up with your partner, because you feel jealous when your partner does X with a person of sex Y, and your partner wants to do X with people of sex Y, and you don't like controlling your partner and you don't like feeling jealous, so this isn't the relationship for you.

Hey, at least it's an honest response. You've thrown the refrigerator away, and replaced it with a new one.

And that's about where your options end, right?

Wrong. There's another option. You can fix the refrigerator.

In the past, when my partner has done something that's made me feel jealous, I've tried just ignoring it in the hopes that the jealousy will go away, and I've tried telling my partner not to do that thing any more, and neither one has ever really been effective. Nowadays, with a little experience and (I hope) a little more emotional maturity behind me, my response is much different. Were I in your partner's shoes, the conversation would go a bit differently:

I don't have any problem with my partner having a relationship with another man, but I'll continue using that as an example. If I did have a problem with that, the conversation between my partner and I might go something like this:

'I am uncomfortable with this, and for some reason the idea of you playing alone with a person of the same sex as you are is OK with me but the idea of you playing alone with the person of the same sex as I am is not OK with me.

I do not understand these feelings yet, but they seem like they are rooted in some kind of fear (such as the fear that I cannot compete with someone of the same sex as me), or possibly some jealousy. I need to work on this, because I recognize that it is irrational and unjustified. Therefore, it is OK with me if you play with someone of either sex, but I will want to talk to you about it afterward, and analyze my feelings and reactions, and try to understand them so that I can address whatever is causing these reactions. After you are done, I will need some time with you so that we can work together at identifying what is causing this irrational emotional response on my part.'

That's what I mean when I say 'fix the refrigerator.'

The nice thing about doing this is that you can, if you have isolated the emotional response beneath the jealousy and identified positive ways to deal with it directly, end up in a position where you don't feel jealous anymore. Even when your partner does the things that used to trigger the jealousy. You just don't feel jealous any more. You do not need to pass rules banning certain behavior and you do not need to veto someone, because you don't feel jealous anymore.

The downside, though, is that your irrational fear will fight to protect itself; it won't go down easy. The thought process goes like this:

'If my partner does these things with someone of the same sex as me, then I might lose my partner, because someone else might give him the same things I give him. If I lose my fear of losing my partner, I will no longer have a reason to ask my partner not to do these things. If I don't have a reason to ask my partner not to do these things, then my partner will do them, because I know he wants to do them. If my partner does these things, I will lose my partner, because then someone else will give him the same things I give him. So I better not get over my fear, because if I get over my fear, then I won't have a reason to ask him not to do these things, and that means he'll do these things, and that means...I'll lose him!'

And 'round and 'round it goes. You don't want to lose the fear, because you're afraid something bad will happen, and you can't give up the fear of something bad happening because if you do...you're afraid something bad will happen.

Fixing the refrigerator requires a leap of faith. It requires believing, even if your fear is telling you otherwise, that your partner is with you because your partner wants to be with you. If you start with the assumption that your partner wants to be with you, then anything becomes possible—including defeating your jealousy without passing rules.

But you have to start there. You got to take it on faith, even when your fear is telling you otherwise—and believe me, it will.

It also requires communication. I'm not trying to suggest that if you are secure and confident in your relationship, and you don't try to pass rules banning the triggers for feelings like jealousy, that means you'll automatically know what you want. Far from it.

In any relationship, communication is absolutely vital. Maintaining a healthy relationship means talking to your partner about how you feel and where you're at, even when you're feeling negative or destructive things.

But I have found that that works best when the communication is a dialog, not a decree. Rather than saying 'I feel jealous when you do thus-and-such; I hereby forbid you to do thus-and-such,' you say 'I feel jealous when you do thus-and-such. Here's why I feel jealous; these are the things I'm afraid might happen. How can we all work together to address these things?'

Now, if you're on your hands and knees behind the refrigerator with a flashlight in your mouth, you probably don't want your partner trying to pile more food into the fridge while you're working on it, right? So it seems reasonable to say, 'Honey, don't put any more food in there until I fix the problem, 'kay?' And this is exactly what many people will tell you they're doing when they say, 'My partner does something with someone else, and it makes me feel jealous, so I told him not to do that thing any more—but only until I get to the bottom of it and deal with the jealousy.'

All well and good, but you have to be really careful with this approach. If you're not, then what happens is that days turn into weeks, weeks turn into months, you're still uncomfortable with your partner doing whatever it is, months turn into years, and what's actually happened is that you've said you're going to fix the refrigerator but it's still sitting in the corner dripping water all over everything and, effectively, you're just not buying any refrigerated foods anymore.

When dealing with a jealousy or insecurity issue, it's important to differentiate between not wanting to do something because it's uncomfortable, and not wanting to do something because it's actually harmful. Some things are a no-brainer.

People often accuse me of being against rules of any sort in a relationship. Actually, this isn't the case at all; I have rules in all my relationships, and certain standards of behavior that are essential and non-negotiable for anyone who wants to be partnered with me. I do not intend to come across as saying that there should be no rules in a relationship. Quite the contrary; some rules are reasonable and prudent, and some fears are rational and justified.

A trivial example is sexual health. STDs are real. they exist, and they can kill you. Anyone in a sexual relationship of any sort, especially multiple sexual relationships, is well-advised to keep that in mind, and design a minimum standard of behavior for himself and his partners to deal with that risk. In fact, you'd have to be a fool or a madman not to think about STDs when you create your relationship arrangements, and fear of STDs is not only rational, it's downright prudent. Creating rules to protect yourself from this risk is a damn good idea.

Things aren't as clear-cut when you're dealing with emotional risk, however, Fears and insecurities are very, very clever at protecting and justifying themselves, and separating something that is actually harmful from something that's merely uncomfortable isn't always easy. It requires work. It requires examining, with an unflinching eye, what it is you're afraid of and what it is you think will happen if your partner continues doing the thing that makes you jealous. And above all, it requires that you ask yourself, on a regular basis, what is the point of all this?

Many people in the poly community seem to be inherent pessimists, and to have a worst-case scenario of relationship.

What I mean by that is that many people start their polyamorous relationships from the perspective that polyamory itself is inherently destructive, you can't reasonably expect your poly relationships to be healthy and positive, and if you don't ride herd on them all the time and manage your relationships and your partner's behavior strictly, all that will happen is you'll lose everything.

You see this in the language that people use to describe their relationships. 'Well, we do primary/secondary in order to protect the primary relationship.' Protect the primary relationship? Protect it from what? The basic premise is that if you DON'T do primary/secondary, then you'll automatically find yourself in a situation that destroys the primary relationship; after all, if that were not the case, why would you need these structures to 'protect' the existing relationship in the first place? If you believe that you need these rules in order to make sure your needs are met, then what is it that makes you think that another person's needs must automatically come at the expense of your own?

When you start from the default assumption that other relationships are a threat, and you need to manage and control that threat, then of course it makes sense to assume that part of managing that threat means passing rules that place strict controls on your other relationships. But if you start from the default assumption that polyamory is implicitly threatening to your existing relationship, then what the hell are you doing poly for?

But wait, it gets worse! You see, people's behaviors don't spring from a vacuum. People act the way they do for a reason. If your partner's behavior, left unchecked, is disrespectful to you and recklessly disregards your needs, then you don't really solve the problem by placing controls on his behavior. The problem runs deeper than that. And on the contrary, if your partner loves and respects you and wants to do right by your relationship, then you don't need to place controls on his behavior; his behavior will reflect the fact that he wants to do right by you, and does so because he chooses to, not because you make him. As Shelly wrote elsewhere, behavior is an emergent phenomenon.

You don't actually control your partner's heart by controlling his behavior. If your partner's heart is not really with your relationship, making rules won't protect your relationship; if your partner's heart is with your relationship, making rules to protect the relationship is unnecessary.

Let's get back to not putting vegetables into the fridge while it's being fixed. Yes, this is a very, very good idea. It is not always true that a person who says 'not now' actually means 'not ever.' There are many people who say 'not now' because they are, in fact, working on the problem, and sometimes working on the problem takes time.

Here's the thing, though. Working on the problem means working on the problem. It means taking affirmative action toward addressing the underlying jealousy. It means making progress.

What can sometimes happen is that a person can sincerely believe that he wants to address the underlying insecurities or fears behind his jealousy, and he can genuinely imagine a time when he does not have those fears and his partner can do whatever it is that triggers the jealousy. But you aren't going to get from here to there without discomfort. If you wait for a time when you no longer feel uncomfortable, then you'll be waiting forever, and that time will never come, because the very act of working on the fears and insecurities means being uncomfortable. You cannot challenge a fear without exposing yourself to it. You cannot fix the refrigerator until you actually get on your hands and knees and crawl around behind it and start tinkering with the guts of the thing with a flashlight in your mouth, and that's uncomfortable.

If you say 'Don't do this until I feel comfortable with it' and then you don't challenge your discomfort, you are saying 'Don't do this' and sneaking the rule in the back door. If your relationship is broken and three weeks later you're still saying 'No, honey, don't bring any frozen foods home yet, it's still not working,' what kind of progress are you making?

Things can get a little trickier still (this business of romantic relationship is messy, isn't it?) when your partner has done something, intentionally or unintentionally, to damage your trust or to mistreat you in some way. When this happens, it takes time to rebuild trust and to repair the damage, and it's reasonable to expect not to keep doing things which are threatening until you get enough time and distance to separate the damage from mere discomfort.

Of course, I say 'mere discomfort' even though I know full well that that 'mere discomfort' can be an overwhelming tidal wave of jealousy that so completely washes over you that it leaves you shaking and twisted up in agony and unable to do or say or think about anything save for making the feeling go away. Hey, I never said it was easy—only that it's possible, and necessary.

How to become a secure person

Some polyamorous people see polyamory as a path to spiritual enlightenment, believing that polyamory connects them with the universal spirit of the Divine or some such thing.

Me, I'm not terribly spiritual. (Yes, it's true!) I don't see polyamory as a 'spiritual path,' I'm not prone to believing in 'sacred sexuality' as a way to explore my connection with the Universal Cosmic Divine, and my own approach to polyamory (and to life in general) is very practical and hands-on. This is why I do not believe, for example, that love is infinite...but that's a topic for another time.

There is a saying: 'There is no fear in love, but perfect love casts out fear.' I don't believe a word of it. Often, the way it works in practice is quite the opposite. You get rid of fear, and the love follows more easily. The 'getting rid of fear' part, though, is the trick.

And getting rid of fear and insecurity makes life better. Ultimately, dealing with fears and insecurities is something that must be done; a person can deal with them by hiding from them, deal with them by rearranging his life around them, or deal with them by destroying them completely, but not dealing with them generally isn't an option. And frankly, with the amount of time and effort people invest in hiding from their fears or building their lives around their fears, just eradicating them to begin with is actually less effort in the long run.

This page is about practical, ordinary ways to deal with fear and insecurity, and become self-confident and self-assured.

Don't always assume you can trust your feelings

Fear is deceptive. Fear will attempt to justify itself. Often, you can think of your fears as though they were living creatures of their own; they will fight to protect and defend themselves, just like any other living thing.

Fear is tricky because it can color and distort the way you see the world. You will often see (or, sometimes, fabricate) things that support your fear while totally missing things that contradict your fear. On top of that, when you are afraid, you tend to project that feeling into the past, remembering most strongly those things that confirm your fear; and into the future, and believe, if only subconsciously, that this is the only way you will ever respond to this kind of situation, and no other response is possible.

Fear tends to wither and die if you drag it out into the light, though. I'm personally a big fan of marching into the closet, grabbing the biggest and ugliest monster in there by the tail, and then dragging it out and going toe-to-toe with it. Fears gain strength when you let them hide in the shadows, and lose strength when you examine them and confront them head-on.

So. I'm going to start with a hypothetical situation, and lay out a plan for conquering a fear, step by step. Different fears express themselves differently, and fears and insecurities can manifest in many ways, but the same tools can be used for dealing with them all. For the sake of example, I'll start with a fairly common response I've seen in poly relationships many times: you have a partner, your partner has another partner, and you feel insecure or jealous when you see them together in a romantic context, like when you see them kiss.

Ready? Here we go!

First, look beneath the surface

Before you can do anything else, you must figure out what lies at root of the response. This is the first and most critical of all tools for dealing with fear or insecurity. Insecurities, jealousies, and fears are often composite emotions—emotions made of other emotions. You can't confront the fear until you understand what lies beneath it.

Say, for example, you see your sweetie kissing someone else, and that brings up a negative emotional response— jealousy, fear, whatever. Look at that fear! (Yes, I know this is difficult; when you're in the grip of a negative emotion, all you want to do is make it stop, right now, by any means necessary.) Examine what it's telling you. Why do you have that response? Is it because you believe that you can't compete with the other person? Is it because you're afraid your lover may find you wanting? Is it because you're afraid your lover will leave you, or want you less, or prefer someone else's company? Try filling in the blanks: 'If my lover kisses another person in front of me, then the bad thing that will happen is _____.' 'If this keeps happening, then it means _____.' 'If my lover really loves this other person, then _____.'

Further down the rabbit hole

Once you have an idea of what it is that underlies the fear, keep following it down the rabbit hole. For example, let's say that you have a negative emotional response when you see your partner kiss someone else, and you figure out 'I am afraid that that other person might kiss better than me, and my partner might want that other person more than me.' Well, now figure out what's underlying that fear. Is it rooted in fear of abandonment? Low self-esteem? Fear of competition? Fear of loss? What is it you're afraid that means? Why do you believe that the other person might kiss better than you—and more to the point, why do you think that's even relevant?

Disassemble! Disassemble!

When you've done that, you've made a lot of progress. For example, let's say you have a negative emotional response when you see your partner kiss someone else, you've figured out that the response is caused because you fear that if your partner's other partner is a better kisser than you, you will lose something, and you've figured out that this is rooted in the idea that if your partner's other partner is more pleasing to him, your partner will want to be with that other person and not with you.

Okay, now we're getting somewhere! The root of the response is fear of abandonment. Now you need to take that fear apart. This is what I mean when I say 'drag the fear out of the closet and go toe-to-toe with it.' You need to disassemble the response, and figure out whether or not it's valid.

One way to do this is to examine the assumptions about your relationship that your fear reveals. Do you believe that your partner is with you because of the way you please him in bed? Do you believe that if your partner finds another person more sexy or more pleasing, you may lose some or all of your relationship? Are those beliefs founded? Is it possible that your partner is with you for reasons besides those? What might those reasons be? What value do you add to your partner's life? Does your partner value you for the way you please him, or for who you are? Is it even meaningful to say that one person can replace another?

Now, the danger in doing this is that sometimes, you may find your fear really is justified. Not all fears are irrational. There are people in the world who are only with someone for a lay, and will move on as soon as they find a better fuck. It could very well be that in this hypothetical situation, this is the case. If so, so be it. The best way to keep from being disillusioned is not to have any illusions in the first place; if your partner is only with you for a lay, then this is the kind of thing you should know.

But more likely, you will find that when you do this, your fears fall apart. When you examine your relationship with your partner, you will likely find that, no, you add value to your partner's life in a myriad of ways, large and small, and that even if your top-level fears are realized and your partner finds someone better in bed than you (or whatever), it does not mean you will lose your partner.

How do you get to Carnegie Hall?

At this point, I'm going to digress a bit and talk about what it means to be a 'fearful person' or an 'insecure person' or a 'jealous person.'

I've talked to a lot of people who say things like 'Oh, I could never be polyamorous; I'm just a jealous person'—as if being a jealous person were some matter of genetics, something over which we all have no control, like being born with blond hair or...well, no, people actually think they have more control over their hair color than over their own conceptions about themselves, which is interesting.

Let's say you went to a piano concert. Would you say that the pianist up on the stage was 'just a good pianist,' as if that's all there was to it? Hell, no—and if you did, she'd likely punch you. You get to be a good pianist by long, hard practice. A good pianist is made, not born.

The same is true of being a secure person—or an insecure person. People are accomplished at being insecure because they practice being insecure. They practice diligently, every day, for years; it's no wonder they're good at it.

You practice being insecure every time you let yourself think 'Oh, I'm not good enough for that' or 'Oh, my partner doesn't really want to be with me' or 'Oh, I don't deserve that' or whatever.

After a time, this way of thinking becomes natural and effortless. A pianist who has practiced enough does not consciously have to move each finger to the proper key; after a while, they find the keys by themselves, without conscious effort. A person who practices being afraid or insecure soon becomes very natural at it; you find the things to support your fear, you learn the tools to reinforce your fear, without consciously thinking about it.

The same is true of self-confidence and security. These are things you practice; practice them enough, and they become totally natural, a part of who you are.

Building better habits

So back to dealing with fear. Once you've deconstructed your fear, discovered what it's rooted in and taken those roots apart, once you've found a list of things that discredit your fear, it's simply a matter of reaching for those things that your partner values in you and that you add to your partner's life whenever the fear raises its head. The thing about fear and jealousy and insecurity is that these things are a lot like like playing a piano; they represent ways of looking at the world that improve with practice. Just as practice can make a person into a highly accomplished pianist, so does practice turn someone into a highly fearful or highly jealous person. And on the contrary, practicing discrediting your fear, developing the mental habit of staring down your fears and insecurities and saying 'No, you're wrong, and here's why' whenever they stir, will make you accomplished at feeling self-confident and secure.

Once you understand why your fear is flawed, you simply have to train yourself to stop reinforcing it, and to reinforce the feelings of value and security instead. This will feel awkward and unnatural at first, just as learning to play the piano feels awkward and unnatural at first. But you become good at what you practice. If you practice being afraid, you get good at it; if you practice being courageous and fearless, you get good at that.

When I feel something that makes me feel insecure or fearful, I tend to want to push on that thing. So to take my hypothetical example, if I were to feel an unexpected negative reaction at seeing a partner kiss someone else, rather than try to hide from it or to tell my partner not to do it, I would instead tell her, 'I feel this way when I see this, so when you do this when I'm around, I may want to talk to you about those feelings later.' I certainly would not expect her not to do it in front of me; I believe that approach is the way away from courage, and would simply make the fear stronger.

When you push on the things that make you afraid— when you deliberately expose yourself to those things— you rob them of their power. On the other hand, when you give in to those fears, or (worse yet) when you pass relationship rules designed to hide the things you're afraid of—'No kissing when I am around!'—you reinforce those fears, and you allow them to control your life. Building your life around your fears is not an effective strategy for leading a happy life; and maneuvering your partner's behavior around your fears is not a good strategy for building a happy relationship.

Three easy steps to self-confidence

How do you practice being self-confident? How do you make all this theory happen? In three steps, just like the title says, of course!

- **Step 1:**

First, understand that you have a choice. You did not choose your past experiences, of course; you did not choose to have people make fun of you back in the fifth grade, or have a past partner who told you you weren't good enough, or whatever…but you did have a choice about believing these things and internalizing them, and right now you do have a choice about continuing to believe them, or changing the things you believe about yourself.

The single hardest thing to do if you want to change your self-image is to realize that it is a choice. Once you've made that step, the rest is easy.

- **Step 2:**

Once you understand that you have a choice over the way you feel, the next part is simple. Choose to act like someone who is self-confident, even though you are not. Remember, you control your actions; you control your body; you can choose to act self-confident and act secure even if you don't feel it. You will feel uncomfortable, of course; your feelings will try to get in the way of your actions. Acting self-confident will feel phony and forced at first. You will obsess, going over in your mind all the imaginary reasons why you shouldn't be acting this way, you need to be afraid or insecure instead. You still have a choice. You still control your actions. You can choose to act confident even though it feels uncomfortable.

- **Step 3: Practice.**

You become good at whatever you practice. A person who is insecure becomes very good about being insecure because he practices being insecure every day, 7 days a week, 365 days a year. You practice being insecure by thinking about those old insults you heard in fifth grade, remembering them, believing them, telling yourself they are true. You practice being insecure by going over in your mind all the reasons you are not good enough to be with your partner, and imagining how easily he could abandon you if he just wakes up and realizes how worthless you are. You practice being insecure by making lists of everything that is wrong with you.

People who are secure practice being secure. It's no different, really. To practice being secure, stop thinking about all those old insults—when they come into your mind, tell yourself firmly, 'No, these are false, and I choose not to believe them anymore. Why should I believe people who do not like me?' When you find yourself thinking about all the things that are wrong with you, stop, and say, 'No, these are wrong, and here is why. Here is a list of things that are good and sexy about me instead.' (Corny as it sounds, keeping a written list of things you like about yourself in your pocket helps.) When you find yourself thinking of all the reasons your partner does not really want you, or all the reasons some other person is better than you, stop yourself and say 'No, this is false.'

If you practice the piano every day and then one day start playing the harp instead, it will feel uncomfortable and awkward and unnatural, and you will not feel at first like you are making any progress. Do it anyway. You get good at something by practice. You want to be a confident, secure person? Practice being confident and secure, in your words and in your actions.

When you do this, even though it feels uncomfortable and even though you do not want to, you will find that your insecurity goes away remarkably quickly. It doesn't actually take very long to become more secure.

If you want to become secure without ever thinking or doing things that are uncomfortable for you, though, forget it; it will never happen. In order to change your image of yourself, you have to understand that changing the way you act and the way you think is always uncomfortable at first.

Chapter Seven

Communication in Relationships: Is it really important?

Life is constantly influenced by various encounters which can later become treasured relationships. With this, one must realize the significant contribution of communication in order to make these relationships last.

Poor communication results in disagreements and misunderstandings. These factors can turn to anger and distance thereby putting a gap between two parties and staining the relationship. Whenever you go through conflicts that can trigger broken relationships, make sure to take action before it's too late. Do not hesitate to communicate; instead choose to keep in touch and settle the issue right away. Here are some ways to enjoy a very good relationship through effective communication.

Concentrate on the problem and not on the person or the past. In times of conflicts, it is tempting for anyone to bring up the past, especially when it seems to be related to the current situation. Sadly, giving in to this temptation clouds the issue, attacks the other person and worsens the matter. It is best to stay focused on the real issue and avoid bringing up past hurts and other related topics. Deal with the present problem, understand each other and search for a solution.

Own your mistakes. Taking responsibility for your mistakes is classified as your strength. An essential part of effective communication is accepting that you have wronged someone. Normally, the parties involved in conflicts have their share of flaws. Identify what is yours and admit it - this simple act diffuses the problem, becomes a good example at the same time shows maturity.

Not 'you' - try using 'I' statements. Instead of saying, 'This is all your fault!' resolve in expressing your true feelings. You can say, 'I am hurt and frustrated every time this happens.' Statements such as these are less accusatory and display less defensiveness. As a result, the other person sees things in a more positive perspective rather than feeling confronted.

View things through the other party's eyes. One's initial reaction when faced in trying times is to defend himself. People want to be heard and understood thereby focusing on how they view things and giving less attention to what the other person has to say. If you do the other way around and look from the other side, you will discover that you can actually explain your side much better and solve the issue sooner than you expected.

Entertain feedback, whether positive or negative. Most of the time, people assume they are listening but in fact, they are thinking about their next statements once the other person is done talking. Effective communication involves two ways - listening and sharing your ideas. Listen carefully, reflect and respond accordingly.

Respond to comments with understanding.Negative comments can easily make a person wanting to retaliate. It is true that criticisms can be difficult to accept as they can be exaggerated. At certain times, these negative comments can be overemphasized due to the person's rise of emotions. When in situations like these, it is essential that you respond with considerations on how the other person feels. Understand why he is acting that way and gather all valuable information that can fix the problem.

Seek help from others. If you feel you have tried all possible ways to solve the conflict and yet you see no improvement, probably it is time to ask somebody to intervene. The person is ideally someone you both know and highly respect. There should be a different impact when another person discusses the issue without taking any of the side and looks at the problem with fair judgment.

Establish a better and stronger relationship.Whenever a conflict is resolved, aim to take your relationship to the next level. Problems and trials, although may be hard to go through, are among the best reasons why people have better and stronger relationships.

Good communication does not belong to skills that you can master overnight. Rather, it is a learning process where you have all the opportunities to grow. Excellence in communication may be hard to achieve but practice can make you effective in your relationships. Expect to commit mistakes but never intend to do so. If you are looking forward to a closer bond with people around you, simply open your communication lines. You will be surprised to receive the rewards of lifelong relationships.

Communication as the Number One rule of polyamory

'Communication is rule #1 of a polyamorous relationship.'

It's something you'll hear in the poly community so often it's become a mantra. And rightly so; communication is arguably the single best indicator of the health of any romantic relationship, monogamous or polyamorous. A relationship that lacks good communication is built on a foundation that's fundamentally flawed, and a relationship whose members lack good communication skills is a relationship that has problems from the very beginning.

Few people really talks about how to build good communication, though, and that's unfortunate, because good communication is trickier than it sounds. There's more to communication than opening your mouth and saying what's on your mind. Effective communication starts with understanding what's on your mind, particularly if you're trying to solve a problem. It's not just enough to say 'I feel uncomfortable about this' or 'I'm feeling upset about that' or 'I don't want you to do this;' real communication requires understanding what's at the root of those feelings and desires.

Now, hold on, smart guy! If I'm feeling something, I should be able to say so, without all this analysis crap!

Of course. But once you've said what's on your mind, what comes next?

There are people who believe it ends there. 'I've said what I have to say; now it's up to my partner to behave accordingly.' This isn't communication; in fact, this closes the door on communication, because it gives your partner no way to continue, short of doing whatever it is you want him to do.

Communication is about increasing understanding. If you simply say 'This is how I feel' and leave it at that, the conversation is done, and you're not really increasing understanding, because your partner still has no idea why. In fact—

Hang on. I've said what I'm feeling and what I want my partner to do; who cares why?

You should, for one. Let's start with the most obvious first: if your partner does not understand why you feel the way you do, your partner may just end up violating the spirit of the rules without breaking the letter, because he does not understand what the rules are supposed to do.

But let's step back a little from that. It goes beyond simply experiencing an emotion you don't like and then letting your partner know about it so that he can stop doing whatever it is that's leading to your emotion. If you do not understand why you feel what you feel, you may not be able to get a handle on what might change those feelings. It might seem obvious at first glance; 'I get jealous when my partner takes someone else to my favorite restaurant, so if my partner stops taking people there, I won't be jealous anymore.' But feelings are really sneaky, complicated things, and the actions that trigger a feeling may not actually be as directly tied to the feeling as you think. What might just happen is you might just find that you still feel jealous even if your partner promises never to take anyone to that restaurant again, and all that's happened is those feelings are now triggered by something else.

If you don't understand your feelings, then it's pretty damn tough to say with certainty what you or anyone else can do to address them. In fact, as I was about to say, often the roots of feelings and emotional reactions aren't obvious at all, and if you don't understand the problem, it's really difficult to come up with a solution with any real chance of success.

You're telling me that I don't even know what I'm feeling?

No, I'm saying that if you don't make an active effort to understand your feelings, you won't know why you're feeling what you're feeling. And if you don't know why you're feeling what you're feeling, it gets pretty hard to have a dialogue with your partner about it, and it gets even harder to come up with a plan of action based on it.

Not all feelings are true. You may feel something so strongly that you know for a fact that what you're feeling is absolutely right and perfectly justified, know it more surely than you know your own name—and still be wrong. Only by looking at your feelings can you understand the heart of where they come from, and only by understanding them can you really be sure they are appropriate and justified.

Remember what we're talking about here—dialog. You talk to your partner, your partner talks to you, you each come away with a deeper understanding of one another, and that deeper understanding is what helps you solve problems, right?

And solving problems is a lot easier if your partner understands what's going on in your head, which is a lot easier if you understand what's going on in your head. In fact, it very well might be that if you and your partner both have a clear idea about why you're feeling what you're feeling, you might find a better solution than the most obvious one! Saying 'I'm feeling jealous so I want you to stop doing X' is a decree, not an honest attempt at communication; it closes the door to further discussion. Saying 'I'm feeling jealous, and I think this is why, and this is what I've observed to trigger those feelings' opens the door not only to further discussion, but to finding some kind of solution that might not have occurred to you.

Communication is already difficult enough even if you understand perfectly whatever it is you're trying to talk about; if you don't understand what you're talking about, forget it.

What do you mean, communication is difficult enough? If I'm talking to my partner, and—

If you're talking to your partner honestly.

Okay, fine. If I'm talking to my partner honestly, and—

Funny you should mention honesty. That's another one of those little things that's trickier than it sounds. Honesty, like understanding, begins at home, with yourself. In order to be honest with another person, you must first be honest with yourself, and part of that means recognizing and acknowledging the reality of who you are and the reality of your situation.

This is true across the board, but it's most especially true in very difficult situations such as mono/poly relationships. For example, if one person has it somewhere in the back of her mind that she's monogamous, she wants a monogamous relationship, and if she can just make things complicated enough on her partner, her partner will give up this poly stuff, but she hasn't really quite admitted to herself that that's what she's doing, then any effort at communication is already undermined. She may believe she's talking openly and honestly with her partner, but because she hasn't really admitted to herself what's going on, she's not really being honest with him.

And before you say I'm picking on the monogamous person unfairly, if a polyamorous person is seeking multiple relationships because he has a deeply seated but quite subtle fear of commitment or vulnerability, and so he's driven to avoid uncomfortable intimacy by starting new relationships over and over, then he's not going to be able to communicate honestly with any of his partners about what he wants or what his relationship goals are, because he hasn't admitted that to himself yet.

And while we're at it, a quick word on honesty and lies:

A lie is any conscious, deliberate attempt to deceive or mislead. Many people will find all kinds of ways to justify lying, especially indirect lying; 'Oh, I haven't told him about thus-and-such because he hasn't asked,' or 'Oh, I haven't told her anything that is not factually untrue, so I haven't lied.'

A good liar tells lies that are mostly true; a masterful liar can lie without ever uttering a single falsehood.

Consider these examples. If I tell someone 'I will be at your house at two o'clock,' and at one forty-five I'm struck by a bus, I have not lied; I did not show up at two o'clock, but it was not my intent to mislead that person. If, on the other hand, I am having an affair and cheating on my partner while at my office, and my partner asks me 'Did you cheat on me today?' and I respond 'I was at my office all day,' I have lied; I have given an answer calculated to mislead my partner into drawing the wrong conclusion.

Okay, then...I've looked inside myself, I understand what I'm feeling and I understand the reality of my situation, and I'm not going to lie, directly or indirectly. Now I'm home free, right?

Not only are you not home and dry, you're not even home and vigorously toweling off yet. It gets more complicated.

Huh? I understand myself; I understand what I need to say, I just have to say it!

And your partner needs to understand it, which is more than just a matter of speaking the same language. Remember, your partner has no way to crawl behind your eyes and see the world the way you do; your emotional reality is just an abstraction to your partner, and everything he knows about it comes only from what you tell him.

Indeed, two people can have radically different emotional realities, and bridging that gap is not easy.

So. Let's assume you're honest, you know yourself, and you're sincere about this whole communication thing. There's still plenty of things to go wrong; here's a few things you should keep in mind:

Don't assume that your partner would feel the same way you do if he were in your shoes. 'Well, just think about how I feel!' isn't terribly helpful; your partner may be thinking about how you feel, but if he doesn't feel the same way himself and wouldn't react the same way in your position, what he's thinking is likely to be off base. Tell him how you feel—and tell him why.

Don't take somebody else's word for what your partner is doing or thinking, and don't rely on someone else to tell your partner what you're doing or thinking. Talking through a proxy never works. Seriously. Everyone has a slightly different worldview and a slightly different interpretation of events; what you're hearing when you're talking through a proxy is your partner's ideas filtered and interpreted through someone with a different take on reality, and there's really no way around that.

Don't slam the door. Door-slamming behavior can be literal or figurative; it's anything that closes off dialog, as in walking out of the room and slamming the door, or simply cutting off your partner. It doesn't come just from issuing decrees; it comes any time you don't want to hear what your partner has to say or don't give your partner the opportunity to respond to what you have to say. And along the same lines:

Don't make a habit of issuing ultimatums. An ultimatum leaves no room for negotiation; like a decree, it cuts off further dialog. Ultimatums, if they are necessary at all, are an absolute last resort, best reserved for a situation that, if it does not change, will definitely end the relationship. An ultimatum is appropriate only in the most extreme and dire of circumstances: 'get help with your drinking problem or I will not be able to stay.'

Don't get caught up in your own assumptions or your own interpretations. This one is particularly devious, because we all tend to assume that what we think and what we see is the 'right' way to think and the 'right' way to see a situation. But your interpretation of something may differ dramatically from your partner's; it's helpful to get into the habit of mentally asking yourself 'What if I'm wrong?' whenever you think you've got something all figured out.

So even if you understand yourself, you understand what you have to say, and you understand why you feel the way you feel, you still have to be careful.

Wow. Okay, so now I've got it licked...

Not quite. There's still the 'blue fish tuba' effect.

The who what? That makes no sense!

Precisely.

Each of those words individually has a simple meaning, but put together in that order, they make no sense. Often, that's what it seems like to someone who does not share your conceptual worldview.

Communication on the one hand is quite robust, but on the other hand is very fragile; it's robust in the sense that language is quite resilient, but it's fragile in the sense that when you are talking to someone whose philosophical worldview is vastly different from yours, then when you try to explain a difficult concept, your words end up sounding like 'blue fish tuba.' It's the concept that's difficult; if the concept itself is foreign to your listener, then the words stop making sense.

For example, take a person whose idea of relationships is 'commitment means exclusivity.' If you tell such a person 'It is possible to be committed to more than one person at a time,' your words sound like 'blue fish tuba,' because the concept of commitment inherently implies exclusivity to that person—saying 'commitment to two people' is about like saying 'the tuba was so huge it was tiny.'

Explaining a foreign concept to someone is particularly frustrating; often, you need to invest a great deal of work in isolating and identifying the places where your conceptual frameworks don't overlap, and then carefully building a bridge between those different conceptual frameworks.

In the example of a person to whom 'commitment' means 'exclusivity,' this means trying to find a way to express the concept that it is possible to be committed to more than one thing at the same time; until you can communicate this concept, everything you say about commitment will sound like 'blue fish tuba.'

Wow. This does get tricky. But once I'm over that hurdle, I'm home free…right? Right?

Um…no. It still gets complicated…because there's the second half of communication, which I haven't even mentioned yet, and that is listening.

Listening is active, not passive. If you're planning out the next thing you're going to say, you're not listening. If you're looking out the window, you're not listening. If you're so wrapped up in trying to make your point that you've forgotten your partner is also trying to make a point, you're not listening.

And listening is confounded by the fact that people rarely remember the exact words told to them; they remember only the concepts. Which means if you misunderstand the concept, you're totally screwed.

One of the most common problems with communication from the listener's point of view is the problem of interpretation; if you think you've understood your partner, you may find that you assume your interpretation is the only correct one, and if you're wrong, you may find yourself resistant to what your partner was actually trying to say.

But I am listening to my partner—it's just that my partner isn't listening to me!

And from your partner's perspective, it's the exact same situation, only with the pronouns reversed.

It's easy to feel like you're not being heard when you're not hearing your partner; you end up in a competition to speak your piece and forget about the fact that communication is about mutual understanding. If you don't understand your partner, you can't communicate with your partner; and here's where things can get all kinds of cattywumpus if you aren't paying attention: you need to understand where your partner is coming from even if you personally happen to believe your partner is irrational, mistaken, or flat-out wrong.

You can't ignore what your partner is saying just because you believe your partner is being irrational or bullheaded; for starters, the emotional reality for your partner is different than it is for you, and furthermore, it just might be possible that your partner is trying to express something that doesn't fit within your conceptual framework, and you are the one suffering from the 'blue fish tuba' effect.

If you want to understand your partner, there are a few things you need to keep in mind:

Don't assume that you already know what your partner is going to say. Listen to what your partner is saying instead.

Don't assume that you can disregard what your partner is saying, thinking, or feeling simply because you don't happen to believe that those thoughts or feelings are justified, or because they aren't what you would think or feel in your partner's shoes.

Don't jump the gun; don't assume that you know where your partner is going with an idea and cut him off before he gets there. He just might surprise you.

It's inevitable that you will project your own feelings and your own attitudes on what someone else says to you; we do tend to interpret the world in light of our own experiences and our own attitudes. Be aware of that. Try, as far as is possible, to listen to what your partner says from outside your own preconceptions. This means, among other things, not making assumptions about the reason your partner is saying something and not reading more into your partner's words than is warranted; if your partner says, 'Would you like to go out to dinner tonight?' don't read into that question a statement ('I don't like cooking for you anymore').

One of the greatest enemies to communication is an exaggerated sense of insult or injury. If you feel wronged by your partner, it's quite likely you're not going to be particularly inclined to hear what he has to say, and it's also likely you will interpret everything he does say in the worst possible light. Do not assume that every perceived slight is intentional; do not assume that someone has acted out of spite or malice if there is another possible explanation; do not assume that your own grievance is always justified; do not assume that your feelings are the only ones that are relevant.

I don't have an exaggerated sense of insult—my partner hurt me!

When you feel your partner has hurt you, it can feel just, right, and reasonable to want to lash out at your partner. After all, your partner deserves it, right? He hurt you, right?

Whenever you feel this way, though, it becomes very, very important to keep two things in mind:

1. Just because I feel bad doesn't mean somebody else did something wrong.

2. Just because I feel good doesn't mean I'm doing the right thing.

When you feel attacked, slighted, or hurt, you can very easily slip into believing that you are justified in attacking your partner. That makes your partner feel attacked, and she will then feel justified in attacking you back. You may feel hurt, but that does not make it OK to attack your partner...and if you do, you will probably shut down all hope at productive communication, and with it all hope of solving the problem.

Just because I feel bad doesn't mean somebody else did something wrong. Just because I feel good doesn't mean I'm doing the right thing. Remember those two things, before you escalate an argument.

Okay, I understand active listening, and I can stay reasonable even if I think my partner is being unreasonable...but it doesn't help if my partner won't talk to me.

True.

There are many reasons why your partner might not want to talk to you. A partner who doesn't want to talk to you creates serious problems; the best measure of the health of a romantic relationship, as I've said before, is the quality of the communication in it.

Some of the reasons a partner might not want to talk to you are reasons you can't control. But many of them are. The single best thing you can do to help your partner open up to you is to make it clear that it is safe for him to open up to you.

Communication is a learned skill. Many people are afraid of talking openly and honestly with their partners because they are embarrassed by the things they feel or the things they want, or they are afraid of the way their partners will respond, or they are afraid to make themselves vulnerable to their partners, or they are afraid of being laughed at or rejected by their partners.

You can do a lot to reassure your partner that this will not happen—that you will not mock, reject, laugh at, or think poorly of your partner no matter what he says. Even if the things he says are things you don't want to hear.

But when you tell your partner that it is safe to talk openly and honestly with you, make sure you mean it. The worst thing you can possibly do is tell your partner 'It's okay, you can tell me anything' and then punish your partner or react badly to your partner when he does talk to you!

Geez. Um—anything else?

Glad you asked!

Once you've got all that stuff down, you're almost there. There are a few more points to consider, though, which I'll put in another of those handy lists:

When your relationship involves more than two people, it is essential that all the people involved be a part of your communication, especially in any situation that impacts everyone involved. Even if you divide your relationships into 'primary' and 'secondary' relationships, a secondary partner still has a right to be included.

Don't call the other person names. Seriously. This should be obvious, but it bears repeating anyway. 'You're a selfish prick' is not a good communication tactic; 'I feel neglected because you're paying more attention to your job than to me' is better; 'I'm feeling neglected, but here are some things which might help to make me valued' is better still.

Communication works best when it's an ongoing process. It's not something you do when things get out of hand; it's something you do all the time. Don't wait for small problems to become big problems before you talk about them! Keep checking in with your partner all the time; make it a habit.

Be proactive. If something arises that you need to talk about, talk about it. Often, it might seem tempting to just let it slide, or to wait for 'just the right time' to bring it up...don't. Communication works when it is proactive; even though it can sometimes seem uncomfortable or even frightening to bring up something that bothers you or that is affecting you in your relationship, you need to do it anyway. Anyone can have good communication skills when communication is easy; it's how you communicate when it's difficult that counts.

Interrupting your partner is rude. It also stops dialog. Remember that the things you feel are important, but they are not matters of fact. Feeling neglected does not necessarily mean you are being neglected! Distinguish between matters of emotional response and matters of fact; your emotional responses are important, and your goal when you feel something is wrong should be to find a way to address that feeling, but don't assume that everything you feel is necessarily true. It's possible to feel threatened when you're not actually being threatened; it's possible to feel neglected when you're not actually being neglected—you get the picture. That goes back to the first point; understand your feelings.

If you keep having discussions about the same thing over and over again, then you're clearly not addressing the problem. When you solve a problem, let it go; don't keep dragging it up.

Communication is a learned skill. Like all learned skills, it becomes easier and more natural with practice. When you're dealing with the problem of communicating a concept or philosophical idea that's foreign to your partner, patience is the name of the game; you may have to explain the same concept sixteen different ways to make it understood.

Ask for feedback. Invite a response to what you say.

An argument occurs because a problem exists in a relationship. Your partner is not your adversary; you both have the same goal, which is to solve the problem. Fixing blame isn't helpful to that goal. However, having said that:

Take responsibility for your decisions (and the consequences, even the unintended consequences) of those decisions. Acknowledge what you've done; if you've done something wrong, say so!

If you're thinking of ways to argue with something your partner said, you're not listening. For Pete's sake, pay attention.

Don't exaggerate, embellish, or make blanket statements that are over the top: 'You never consider my feelings at all!' 'Never? Not even once?' 'Well, you sometimes don't...' A better approach: 'I feel like my feelings aren't getting the consideration they're warranted; here's something you can do to make me believe you're respecting my feelings.'

Chapter Eight

How to quit worrying and love your partner's other partners

Meeting a lover's other lover presents a host of opportunity for cooperation or defection. You can reach out to the other person and try to make that person feel welcome; you can be closed up and defensive to that person; you can even be actively hostile to that person. And, of course, your lover's lover has similar choices.

Reaching out to someone makes you vulnerable. If two people both reach out to one another, then things will tend to go more smoothly; but if one person reaches out and the other is defensive or hostile, the consequences for the person who reaches out can be pretty dire. A strictly rationalistic approach might suggest that the best strategy is to be defensive, because if you're defensive, you have nothing to gain but nothing to lose either, whereas if you reach out, you might gain something—but you might lose a great deal, as well.

And there's no question that your expectations about the other person, and your behavior upon meeting that other person, can easily become a self-fulfilling prophesy.

Suppose you start out, prior to the meeting, by believing that your partner's new love is a conniving, self-centered bitch (or bastard), determined to undermine your relationship and to take your partner away from you. If you go into your first meeting with this belief, I guarantee it's going to show. Your partner's other partner is going to be able to tell that you don't trust him (or her), that you're looking for reasons to dislike him (or her). So that person is likely to behave defensively, even if the first impulse might otherwise have been to reach out to you. You look at the defensive reaction, and say 'See, look! I told you this person was bad news!'

Of course, relationships are complex, and there are all sorts of potential gotchas. People don't always have perfect information. We may see hostility where none is intended. We may believe that we are reaching out to someone else, but we're doing it in a way the other person can't recognize, because we don't have the same communication style. Our attempts at reaching out may be clouded by expectation or fear, or misunderstood as attempts at manipulation. Social interactions aren't as simple as leaving a bag behind the old mill; either the bag is full or it isn't, but social interactions aren't that obvious.

When dealing with a partner's other partner, be nice, don't be envious, withhold cooperation only to the extent that the other person does, and forgive. Given that the rules of this relationships aren't simple, but having the underlisted set of mutual 'rules' in place is one smart way to keep your love life a bit less complicated:

- **Establish how much you want to share with each other:**

Even if you're down with sharing lovers, if you are the jealous type, you're not going to want to hear about what your girlfriend ate at dinner with her other girlfriend, or how much fun your boyfriend had at the wine bar with the third person in your throuple.

You might prefer your partner simply say they're 'going out' when they have a date with someone else and leave it at that. And when it comes to deets about you, tell your partner straight-up whether you're comfortable with her discussing your intimate moments with someone else.

Whether or not you love gushing about your unique relationship, you don't want to share everything with the outside world. Keeping certain things private preserves the moments that are just for you and your partner (think: trips, dates, movies)—it keeps them feeling special and intimate.

- **Respect your partner's partners:**

All relationships call for balance, but ones involving multiple people do even more so, says Greer. One way to keep yours on solid ground? 'Respect your partner's choice in other partners,' she emphasizes.

If you go down the Mean Girl route, your negativity might drive your partner away, or it might convince them that you're not cut out for the relationship you agreed to, one where you're not your partner's focus at all times.

Let me be clear: This doesn't mean you have to be cheerleader for your partner's other relationships—

keeping a respectful distance is a good option, too—but you'd do well to focus on your own relationship and its success.

- **Keep your expectations realistic:**

Of course, Greer doesn't assume you can see into the future and predict breakups, but since multiple personalities, temperaments, and preferences are involved in your polyamourous relationship, your best bet is to remember that you and your partners might not live happily ever after—just like people in monogamous relationships might not.

Being open to the idea of rapid change will soften the blow if and when things suddenly shift. Perhaps your partner 'randomly' decides they'd like to be monogamous with their other partner and breaks up with you, or you realize you're no longer feeling your current partners. No shame, but best to protect your heart by keeping an open dialogue with it.

- **Maintain constant and open communication:**

Because of how quickly the setup of a relationship can change, it's especially important for you and your partners to let each other know the moment you're not into the relationship anymore, when you're no longer happy being with them, or when you're thinking of starting a relationship with someone new.

If you don't, you might feel trapped in an unhappy or unhealthy relationship. And that's never a good thing. Even if you're happy with one person in your poly relationship but not another, that still counts as an unhappy relationship, by the way.

- **Consider your motivations and your partner's:**

Keep in mind that polyamory only works when everyone is on board with it. So if your (formerly only) partner expresses interest in a three- or four-way relationship because they're feeling suffocated by monogamy or they think it will enhance your sex life, for example, don't just give them the green light because you don't want to lose them.

You should only move forward with a polyamorous relationship if you're truly open and willing to give it a try—for you.

However, if you're totally against the idea of non-monogamy, agreeing to letting others into your relationship in an effort keep your partner around becomes a recipe for a disastrous breakup.

If you're a traditionalist and you just can't fathom being happy when your partner is happy with someone else too, you might want to put down this rulebook entirely...and go back to the type of romance that makes you feel loved, supported, and appreciated.

In the end, a quality of a relationship matters way more than the quantity of it.

Printed in Great Britain
by Amazon